THE *Girls'* GHOST HUNTING GUIDE

Stacey Graham

sourcebooks
jabberwocky

Published by Sourcebooks Jabberwocky, an imprint of Sourcebooks, Inc.
P.O. Box 4410, Naperville, Illinois 60567-4410
(630) 961-3900
Fax: (630) 961-2168
www.jabberwockykids.com

Library of Congress Cataloging-in-Publication data is on file with the publisher.

Source of Production: Versa Press, East Peoria, Illinois, USA
Date of Production: April 2012
Run Number: 17729

Printed and bound in the United States of America.
VP 10 9 8 7 6 5 4 3 2 1

Contents

Introduction

DON'T TURN AROUND.

That funny feeling you get right before you turn out the light may not be caused by your creepy little brother after all. It could be something more…interesting.

How can you tell? What makes some of us able to see or hear ghosts, and others—not so much? Everyone has the ability to interact with ghosts, but some of us are more sensitive than others. Learning how to be more conscious of what is going on around you can help you to see what others can't—and experience what others wish they could.

Ghosts have been around longer than the Brussels sprouts in the back of your fridge. With a little help from this book, you may be able to track them and find some answers about how ghosts may interact with the living. Let's go over a little background first.

Energy cannot be destroyed or created. After the body dies, what happens to all that good stuff floating around inside of you? Well, no one knows for sure, though each belief system has its version of where the spirit goes. What interests many ghost hunters isn't the destination of the spirit but the way some spirits get trapped between life and the happily ever after we're all seeking. How did they wander off? Were they turned away for bad hair? Are they sticking around to see what happens next? Or do they simply not know they're dead yet?

Paranormal researchers have a few different theories about why ghosts exist:

To finish business. Some ghosts won't be able to leave until they've wrapped up the loose ends of their life. They may feel the need to tell someone one last time that they're sorry or that there's $20 taped to the bottom of the cat dish.

To give a warning. Others may feel that they can't leave until they've done the best they can to warn loved ones that there is something coming around the bend, and they'd better buckle up.

To return to a place they loved. Sometimes, ghosts have a harder time saying good-bye to a location than your Aunt Annie does to the McDonald's drive-thru.

To avenge their murder or right a wrong. These make the best ghost stories. "Who stole my golden aaaaaaaaaaaarm?"

Confusion. A sudden accident or illness that causes death may confuse spirits into thinking they are still alive, and they will try to reach out for help.

So how do ghost hunters find out what's going on out there? A combination of patience, good timing, and, if they're lucky, floating heads.

Investigating ghosts isn't as glamorous as it appears on television. Long periods of time waiting in dusty rooms or basements for something—anything—to happen can drain the fun out of the experience. But if you're willing to look at ghost hunting as an adventure and help the scientific community with your notes, it's a great way to learn more about the unseen world around you.

Ready? You can turn around now.

QUESTION FROM A FUTURE GHOST HUNTER

ARE GHOSTS REALLY REAL?
Hana K., age 11

There's a lot of chatter in the world about whether ghosts are real or not. I think it depends on how willing someone is to be open to discovering another dimension. Skeptics will tell you it's a bit of hogwash to believe in ghosts, while others believe anything that bumps in the night is absolutely the paranormal. I think it's best to have a healthy dose of skepticism while still be willing to entertain the possibility of ghostly activity. Science has come a long way in helping paranormal investigators zero in on what may be a ghost, but we still have some movin' and shakin' to do before there's any hard proof.

CHAPTER 1

A Ghostly History

WHILE THERE HAVE BEEN written accounts of ghosts scaring the togas off people for millennia, it wasn't until the mid-nineteenth century that the living made a business of chatting to them as mediums. Death was common in households due to war, disease and accidents, but through séances, families could reach out one more time to say good-bye. As mediums became well established in communities, the superstars of the late nineteenth and early twentieth centuries emerged through a combination of smooth talking and a little razzle-dazzle.

KNOCK KNOCK— BOO'S THERE?

How did a thump in the night turn into a new religious movement? Deep in the woods of Hydesville, New York, in 1848, two young sisters named Kate and Maggie Fox heard mysterious rappings coming from the walls of their house. On a cold spring night in

March, Kate, then twelve years old, responded to the tapping by asking it to repeat her actions as she snapped her fingers. When it returned the snaps with thumping noises, her family was amazed. The girls' mother proceeded to ask the phenomenon questions, and the ghost would spell out the correct answer using sounds (one thump for the letter A, two thumps for the letter B, three for the letter C—you get the idea).

Word leaked out in their small community about the haunting, and neighbors gathered to witness the girls communicate with the spirit. The news of their ability to talk to ghosts spread even farther, and a new religion called Spiritualism sprang up and swept the nation. Kate and Maggie developed a following, conducting séances where, for a price, they would give people the chance to say good-bye—and possibly find out where their grandmother hid the silver. Mediums cropped up in nearly every city and small town, each offering to tell death's mysteries.

While Kate and Maggie grew more popular, skeptics made their concerns known. Investigative committees were set up to watch the girls while they performed, even going as far as to hold onto their legs and arms while the raps continued to be heard and felt around the room. The Fox sisters seemed sincere, but were they up to trickery?

Years later, Maggie and Kate wavered back and forth as to how much of their séances were real. Maggie even admitted that the girls started the whole thing as a prank and didn't intend to start a national craze of talking to dead people. No matter the truth, Spiritualism had taken hold of the public's imagination, and those who practice it continue to make up a thriving community of seekers and mediums today.

THE AMAZiNG FLOATiNG MAN

Scotsman D. D. Home (pronounced *hoom*) was perhaps the most well known Spiritualist of his time. Immigrating with his aunt to America at the age of nine, Home's early life was filled with paranormal experiences such as his cradle rocking gently by itself and the ability to predict the death of his cousin while he was only four years old.

Similar to the Fox sisters, Home heard knocking sounds in his Connecticut home by the time he was fifteen. When he shared his visions of his own mother's death, his aunt tossed him out into the street, convinced he had been possessed by the Devil. To make a living, Home began to conduct séances in private homes, developing his "talent" and amazing the guests with his ability to stretch his body nearly 11 inches taller than his height of 5'7" and shrink as much as 7 inches to 5 feet tall. His act didn't stop at needing longer pants either. Phantom accordions would play beneath the table where the participants sat in dimly lit rooms while invisible hands stroked their cheeks.

His sittings became an international phenomenon with patrons such as Napoleon III and his wife, Empress Eugenie, and poets such as Elizabeth Barrett Browning and Robert Browning attending. Robert Browning didn't share his wife's fascination with the man, and he wrote a scathing poem about Home called "Sludge the Medium." But while some may have doubted his ability, no one could prove he was up to no good—his act was seemingly genuine.

Home's most amazing feats involved levitation. Tables rose off the floor, and when men attempted to sit on a table to keep it from lifting to the ceiling, it merely rocked back and forth before settling gently on the ground. He didn't stop with furniture; he lifted the mother of his host while she sat in her chair in a fully lit room in front of a roomful of witnesses. Home once levitated himself a foot off the ground during a séance; when the guests tried to bring him back down, he lifted them as well.

During a sitting at Ashley Place in December 1868, Home outdid his other performances. In a trance-like state, he left the room to open a third-story window in an adjoining room and drifted out to dangle above the street below. Three well-respected men within saw him open the window to the first room from the outside and float back in feet first. This caused a huge media stir for the time, and still, no one has been able to explain how he did it.

Women in Ghost Hunting:
Barb Mallon

WEBSITE: www.BarbMallon.com
EMAIL: office@barbmallon.com

I am clairsentient (I psychically feel), clairaudient (I psychically hear), and clairvoyant (I psychically see), all of which I can do to communicate with people who have died.

GGHG *At what age did you identify that you had a special gift?*

> **BM:** I don't believe my abilities are "special." I've just chosen to use them and have developed and refined them over the years. I equate it to building your muscles—you have to work out to form and refine them. Same with your psychic abilities. But to answer the question, I would say I was in my late twenties when what I was telling people about themselves was validated.

GGHG *What is the process you go through when heading into a trance state?*

BM: The state I go into is a light trance stage—almost like daydreaming. I meditate for about 15 or more minutes, connect to my divine energy and archangels, and then "open" myself up to guides and spirit people.

GGHG *What steps do you take to get to the light trance stage?*

BM:

1. Always, always connect to your own divine energy first. Do a little prayer work, pray the rosary, or just visualize that divine light pouring through you.

2. Take some deep, cleansing breaths.

3. See yourself surrounded with white light, and see a stairway of seven steps going up.

4. Head up the steps, and at the top, see a door.

5. Let go of any negative, insecure, worried, stagnant thoughts, and walk into "your" room.

6. This is your safe room/office. Sit in your comfy chair and feel the love and safety in the room.

7. Invite one of your guides to come in, and get to know it, whether or not you can see, hear, or feel them.

8. When you're done, thank them, leave your room, go down your seven steps, reconnect with your divine energy, and slowly come out of your meditation. Be sure to ground yourself by eating afterward, if you can.

GGHG *What is your favorite personal ghost story?*

BM: I was in Fell's Point, Maryland, doing a Halloween event for a local ghost tour. My family (two sons, one four and one six, and my husband) stayed at the Admiral Fell Inn. I had a horrible time trying to sleep that night and tossed and turned all night long. On the floor, I had my suitcase open so I could just grab what I needed when I needed it. At 4 a.m., I woke up and turned over again toward the floor and saw what I thought was my four-year-old son on his knees, rummaging through my suitcase. I sat up, ready to say, "*Bren!* What are you doing up?" and realized it wasn't Bren. The boy looked at me, saw that I had seen him, and literally disappeared. I sat there dumbfounded and even turned the lights on to check the kids. Everyone was sound asleep. I found out via the *Today Show* just a few days later that the Admiral Fell Inn was one of the top ten most haunted hotels in America. Who was the "resident" ghost? A little boy. Still gives me chills!

GGHG *How can a medium help ghost hunters during an investigation?*

BM: I think they can work together—the medium may be aware of an energy, and the ghost hunter can use the equipment to validate.

GGHG *How does what you do help those left behind?*

BM: I feel my work validates that we don't actually die. Our bodies die, but our consciousness/soul lives on. The coolest thing that comes through in sessions is when a spirit person tells me that they've "heard" the questioner's thought about, say, going back to school or "seen" that the questioner locked his or her keys in the car. The light bulb then goes off for the questioner: "Yes…they *are* still around me and see what I do!"

GHOSTLY PHOTOS

A jewelry engraver from Boston named William Mumler is credited with being the first well-known spirit photographer. An amateur photographer, he developed a photo of himself in 1861 only to discover what looked like the ghost of his cousin sharing the space. After the shock wore off, he realized the potential for expanding his business out of watches and into catering to the demand for Spiritualist keepsakes. Charging $10 a print instead of the usual pennies for a photo, he could guarantee that the likeness of a loved one would show up during a customer's sitting. So how did he do it?

Photography took more than the click of a button, as it does today. The sitter would need to remain motionless for nearly a minute as the film was exposed to the light. If the sitter wiggled, it created a blur or "ghost" outline that could be confused for someone butting into the vacation photos.

The camera plates could be used again in a technique called a double exposure, allowing the photographer to pop in a few extras after the sitter left; this would create the illusion of other figures floating through the scene.

One of the more famous spirit photographs attributed to Mumler was of Mary Todd Lincoln. In the photograph, she is seen sitting with the hands of her husband, President Abraham Lincoln, resting on her shoulders, though he had been assassinated years before the photo was taken.

Business thrived for Mumler until he was arrested for fraud. He was eventually found not guilty for lack of evidence. No one could prove that the photos were not genuine, though his business suffered and never regained the popularity it once held.

Other photographers eagerly took over for Mumler, becoming known as mediums with the ability to bring back spirits to pose in pictures. As the Civil War tore families apart, a photograph of the dead standing next to them seemed to have brought comfort to those left behind. Personally, it would have creeped *me* out.

We may look at these photographs now and wonder how anyone could have been fooled, but photography was still new and shiny back then, and death was frequent due to war and disease. Having the fuzzy image of a loved one sharing a photograph helped prove to some that death was merely a chapter in our lives and not the end of the story.

IS THERE A GHOST-ER IN YOUR TOASTER?

How can you tell if there's a ghost in your house? Sometimes, it's easy to blame a ghost for missing jewelry or eating the last of the potato chips, when it's really something as diabolical as your cat. But when you hear knocking in the walls late at night, are you sure it's bad pipes and not the ghost of the old lady down the street?

YES or NO?

1. Something's funky in the corner, and it's not your gym shoes. Are there smells you can't place, like roses in December?

YES   NO

2. Do electronics turn themselves off and on with not a finger in sight to do the button-pushing?

YES   NO

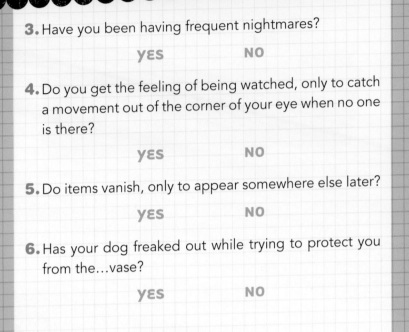

3. Have you been having frequent nightmares?

YES   NO

4. Do you get the feeling of being watched, only to catch a movement out of the corner of your eye when no one is there?

YES   NO

5. Do items vanish, only to appear somewhere else later?

YES   NO

6. Has your dog freaked out while trying to protect you from the…vase?

YES   NO

· · · · · · · · · · · · · · · · · · ·

While it could be something as sinister as that late-night taco run making you jumpy, these may be signals that you have supernatural activity in your house.

Smells: Your sense of smell triggers memories, as well as telling you when dinner is ready. Unusual scents have been reported in cases of haunting, such as cigar smoke at the Whaley House Museum in San Diego, California, and Lemp Mansion in St. Louis, Missouri.

Electronics: There are theories that ghosts try to communicate through the use of electricity or that they drain electromagnetic forces coming from your television and appliances.

Nightmares: When you're in a dream state, ghosts may find it easier to reach out and say howdy. Turn that bad dream into an opportunity to give them a wave back.

Being watched: Very common in active haunted houses, the feeling of being watched is often reported in certain areas of the house only to have the watcher move out of view before anyone can get a good look.

Missing objects: Don't blame your sister for taking your necklace—some ghosts have sticky fingers. Most objects are found later but in a different area of the house—and some never return at all.

Pets: It may not just be the phase of the moon! Some animals react to things that we cannot see by barking or hissing at a certain point in a room or refusing to enter some areas, while other pets will "watch" activity by tracking it with their eyes.

Backseat Drivers

An urban legend is a story that may have had a teeny kernel of truth to it—then gets blown up into some giant blob of a legend that takes over Cincinnati. Perfect to share at a sleepover, urban legends will have you wishing everyone a good fright—er, good night.

Phantom Hitchhikers

Hanging around waiting for someone to haunt can get boring, so these ghosts take matters into their own hands. But how can you tell if it's a ghost and not a determined hobo? Phantom hitchhikers travel the roads in these categories:

> Ghosts who appear human and wait on the side of the road for a lift. After they climb in the car, they'll give an address, then disappear when they reach the destination without even a thank you or $10 for gas money.

> Spirits that may have been involved in hit-and-run accidents. They have become residual hauntings, reliving their accidents over and over again by stepping in front of cars—only to vanish.

> Ghosts that deliver warnings of past accidents on that bit of road. They could be signaling a driver to slow down or get help for a crash that happened years ago.

> Young women who interact with men, usually in party situations. The men then find that the women had died many years before.

Ghosts Don't Have Pockets for Bus Fare

Since the 1980s, a young brunette woman has been trying to hitch a ride to Evergreen Cemetery in west Chicago, often being mistaken for a real person. She once climbed aboard a city bus headed downtown. When she was confronted by the bus driver for the fare, she faded right before his eyes.

Resurrection Mary

Back in the 1930s, the Chicago area was hopping, and it gave birth to the legend of Resurrection Mary, named for a gorgeous blonde, blue-eyed ghost whose body is supposedly buried at Resurrection Cemetery. Mary's story began in 1934 when a car killed a young Polish girl, believed to be Mary Bregavy, on her way home from the O. Henry Ballroom (now the Willowbrook Ballroom) after a fight with her boyfriend. A few years later, drivers would see a girl standing in the cold on the side of the road, looking for help. Kindly, one taxicab driver pulled over and offered her a ride. However, when she climbed onto the seat next to him, she gave only a stony stare and a request to drive north on Archer Avenue. With her sudden shout to stop the car soon as they came close to the graveyard, he braked outside of Resurrection

Cemetery. Turning to see if she was all right, he discovered the girl had vanished.

Mary continued to pop up through the next seventy years, frightening people by leaping in front of their vehicles—sometimes fading before their eyes or worse, reliving the night she was struck by a car and leaving drivers horrified that they had killed her. At other times, she would attempt to jump onto the running boards of cars in the 1940s and 1950s, the drivers swerving to escape the woman in the flowing white gown with wild eyes.

Resurrection Cemetery underwent extensive reconstruction in the 1970s and 1980s. One report in 1977 says a man witnessed a woman within the gates of the cemetery trying to pry the bars open with her hands. After reporting the scene to the police so they could help get her out—obviously someone locked in by mistake—they found the iron spindles of the gate scorched and imprinted with small finger-like depressions as they bowed out toward the street.

Ghouls Just Want to Have Fun

Even ghosts like to get down, get funky. There are multiple reports of girls appearing in party dresses and either joining a group of kids on their way to a party or suddenly appearing at a party and becoming friends with one of the young men. In the latter instance, when he offers to take her home, he lends her his jacket due to the cold weather and drops her off at her house. A few days later, he returns for his coat, discovering from the owner of the house that the girl had died years ago on her way home from a party. Curious, he searches for her grave, only to find his jacket draped over the cold stone.

QUESTION FROM A FUTURE GHOST HUNTER

DO GHOSTS ALWAYS APPEAR IN HUMAN OR ANIMAL FORM?
Wynter G., age 12

Ghosts present themselves in different ways. Some see a figure or part of a figure, such as a head, foot, or thumb, while others get a mental picture in their mind as to what's floating down the staircase.

Seeing a full-bodied apparition is very rare. Most ghost hunters I know are more familiar with watching ghosts interact with objects such as lights and radios or communicate by moving items or making sounds instead. Some people are more sensitive to ghosts, so they may be able pick up on ghostly activity more easily than others.

CHAPTER 2

The Ghosts of Goldfish Past

MANY OF US THINK of ghosts as only being human, but there are a rising number of cases where people have experienced an eerie cuddle from an animal companion that has died. My first experience with ghosts happened after the death of my dog, Jake. A few days after his passing, I began to see a flash of his friendly bulk out of the corner of my eye, and I knew that he would never really be gone forever.

Our pets are also great little ghost detectors. Some animals react strongly to a ghostly presence and as you'll see with Maddie from TAPS, their instincts come in handy during investigations.

PARANORMAL PETS

Ever have your face licked by a phantom dog? Silent movie star Rudolph Valentino's Great Dane, Kabar, likes to give visitors a little lovin' when they pass by his grave at the Los Angeles Pet Cemetery in California. While invisible doggie kisses aren't common, people have reported the presence of long-dead cats and dogs that jump on the bed to claim a favorite napping spot or flash in and out of the corner of their eye. Most ghost pets don't stick around for long, however. It's thought they come back to provide comfort to the family they left behind but then move on. It shows that just because the physical body dies, love never does.

Other visions of ghostly animals aren't as cuddly. Numerous stories exist of misty horses galloping across roadways, making drivers swerve, while back in the empty barn, visitors can hear a ghostly whinny as hooves paw at the ground. In the early seventeenth century, a sentry at the Tower of London defended his post against what appeared to be a large bear wandering what is now called the Martin Tower. Since the tower held a large collection of exotic animals, he must have thought one had escaped! Charging at the bear with his bayonet, he passed the blade through the ghost, only to hit the wall. The man died soon afterward from the shock of the experience.

The Ghost Monkey of Athelhampton Hall in Dorset, Great Britain, was a loyal companion to the end. Following the daughter of the Martyn family to a secret room as she took her own life due to an unhappy love affair, the monkey starved to death before the family found them. While the ghost has never been seen, he can be heard scratching at the door and secret passageway that led to the room.

FOUR-LEGGED GHOST HUNTERS

Maddie, a one-year-old, ghost-hunting German Shepherd-Australian cattle dog mix, helps The Atlantic Paranormal Society (TAPS) with its paranormal investigations. She's been trained to pick up on ghostly vibrations more quickly than her human team members, so she's able to lead them to paranormal activity. She's also able to root out any live animals that may be hiding, fooling humans into thinking they are hearing ghosts instead of tiny mouse feet.

Animals are often able to sense atmospheric differences long before we do. If you've seen your dog go a little nutty or your bird pacing his cage right before a storm, you've witnessed them using their highly developed senses to detect changes in the weather. It's those senses, some paranormal investigators believe, that help them see or hear ghosts when humans can't.

Signs your pet is trying to tell you something's hiding in the closet:

💀 Growling or barking at something you just can't see

💀 Refusing to go into certain rooms

💀 Whimpering or other scared behavior

💀 Acting really, really affectionately toward the food bowl. (Oh, wait. That's normal.)

Women in Ghost Hunting:
Tina Carlson

ORGANIZATION: Las Vegas Society of Supernatural Investigations
WEBSITE: www.lvssi.org
EMAIL: tinacarlson@theshadowlands.net *or* tinacarlson@lvssi.org
YEARS AS A GHOST INVESTIGATOR: 14 years

I have experienced ghosts since I was two, when I had a terrible disease that put me into a coma. Ultimately, I think I had a near-death experience, since I have been able to see ghosts ever since. This ability to see ghosts and experience paranormal activity has been passed down through generations on my mother's side. I grew up listening to stories of my grandpa telling us how he talked to "rapping" spirits every night that tapped on his walls while he lay trying to sleep.

I started working on the Shadowlands website almost fifteen years ago, helping people from all over the world with their ghost questions and problems. I enjoy answering the emails, editing the stories, and maintaining my friendships with staff and visitors. The Las Vegas Society of Supernatural Investigations (LVSSI) came about a year or two after I started on the Shadowlands. At the time, Las Vegas did not have an investigation group, and I am proud to have started the first one here.

GGHG *Do you use tools such as dowsing rods? If so, how do you rate their effectiveness?*

TC: I go mostly by my gut feelings, but [my assistants] Nancy Riggs and Matthew Winn are very well versed in using the dowsing rods. The same grandfather who told me stories also used rods to find water when he was younger and was known as a very good water witch. We have gotten very strong responses that later corresponded with history checks on property or information given to us by clients whose houses we were investigating.

GGHG *What's the one tool you wouldn't be without on an investigation?*

TC: My instinct. I have been called an empath, and that ability has kept my team from danger a few times by warning me either that it's time to leave or that I should avoid certain areas.

GGHG *Do you use electronic voice phenomenon (EVP) in your investigations? Do you feel it's an*

*accurate representation of spirit activity or
just coincidence?*

TC: EVP is a pretty big part of our investigations.
Often, we get responses to our questions that are
direct answers, leaving no doubt in our minds that
this is just not a coincidence. However, every bit
of paranormal evidence collected is subjective at
best and can be torn apart by a persistent skeptic.

Screaming Skulls o' Doom

It sounds like a bad horror flick, but England's screaming skulls have been making a nuisance out of themselves since the sixteenth century. The story of how the skulls got there is a little fuzzy, and stranger still—some of these bad boys are regarded as good luck charms for the families.

Usually tucked away on a bookshelf, on the mantel-piece, or stuffed in a box, each skull would supposedly start a ruckus if removed from its comfy resting place until returned. It was reported that aside from the aforementioned screaming, poltergeist-like activity would kick up, and storms might envelop the surrounding area.

Bettiscombe Manor

In 1685, Azariah Pinney traveled to the West Indies, bringing back to his home at Bettiscombe Manor a servant who later became sick and died. His last wish was to have his body returned to his homeland for burial. Not getting the hint, Pinney instead had him buried in the local churchyard. Unfortunately for those living close by, the grave produced moans and screams that echoed through the night, while Bettiscombe Manor's windows swung open wide and slammed shut. Rattling more than the glass, it took a toll on the nerves of the family as well.

Digging up the servant's body, they brought it back

to the manor house, where it decomposed in a barn until only the skull remained. The rest of the bones were scattered by animals. The skull was returned to the house for safekeeping, and all was quiet. Years later, a new owner of Bettiscombe Manor was completely creeped out, and he threw the skull into a pond on the property. The wailing and screaming drove him mad until he retrieved it from the pond and brought it back to its box.

Another owner decided he'd had enough of the infamous skull and buried it in a deep hole, glad to be rid of it at last. In the morning, he arose to find the skull had somehow dug itself out of the earth and returned to the house on its own.

Challenging the legend in 1963, an archaeologist had the skull examined. He determined that it was not a male from the West Indies at all, but the skull of an Iron Age woman most likely found at a nearby settlement called Pilsdon Pen. Why she was screaming is anyone's guess.

Burton Agnes Hall

Sure, the lovely Elizabethan manor house Burton Agnes Hall is serene and peaceful now, but its tale weaves murder and anguish within the stone walls. Early in the seventeenth century, Sir Henry Griffith built the grand home for his three daughters. Anne, the youngest, was a bit of a wanderer, and during one of her walks, she was attacked by vagabonds, who robbed and beat her and left her for dead. After being found and brought back to the hall, Anne fell into a fever, making her sisters promise when she died to keep her head in her beloved home while the rest of her was buried in the churchyard. Most likely squicked out at the thought of this, they agreed, though later, they buried Anne's body with its head firmly attached.

It wasn't long before the family heard terrible screaming echoing through the house, filled with panic and horror. Returning to the churchyard, they dug up the body of their sister and found that the head was already separated from its spine and devoid of flesh. Once the head was brought back as Anne had requested before her death, the screams quieted—until a maid discovered the head in a cupboard and threw it out the window. Really, who leaves a skull in a cupboard?

Anne yelled her head off until the skull was found and brought back into the hall. Future owners of Burton Agnes Hall tried to get rid of it once again by burying it in the garden, only to be met by more screaming. Well, they *had* been warned. It's rumored that the family had the skull placed in a secret spot within the walls and covered over so no one would be tempted to toss poor Anne from her home once again.

CHAPTER 3

Phantom Parties

HAVE A LITTLE DOWNTIME between investigations? Too cold and rainy to hunt for ghosts outside? How about throwing a Phantom Party with your friends? Pick out your favorite ghostly movies and glue a jewel to your forehead to look properly mysterious. Check out the tips on table tipping, and whip up some ghostly goodies to munch on with a recipe for Bloody Muddy Ghost Cookies!

TABLE TiPPiNG

Remember our old friends, the early mediums of Chapter 1? One of the methods they used to communicate with the other side was actually a parlor trick called table tipping. Often demonstrated at séances, table tipping quickly became a popular alternative to counting out the rapped alphabet developed by the Fox sisters—it just took too long to spell out a sentence.

In the early twentieth century, home parties sprang up to try this relatively quick and easy way to chat with the dead instead of using a professional medium. All it took was a dedicated group of three to four people, a small table, and the ability to not freak out when the nightstand started dancing. It was reported in some groups that the table would move by itself across the room as long as the "tippers" were able to keep their hands on its surface. Other times, the table would tip from one leg to another in response to a yes or no question. Some home parties merely heard loud raps from underneath the table, so be prepared!

TRY IT!

TABLE TIPPING

1. Determine how you're going to record the information received: voice recorder, friend who can take notes while not at the table, or videotape.

2. It's easy to get distracted if and when the table starts to move, so have some questions ready if you're trying to reach someone in particular.

3. Find a small table where you and your friends can sit comfortably—getting a response might take a while. Don't try to tip the dining room table; you don't want it landing on your foot if it rises off the ground!

4. Dim the lights to create a spooky mood. Turn off all other noises such as televisions, radios, and little sisters.

5. Table tipping works best if you relax and have fun with the experiment. If you get all stressed out about what might happen, it may not work, and you'll have to try again.

6. Have everyone place their hands on the table and con-centrate on having something happen—moving, tipping, rapping—and ask your question. It works best if hands remain on the table at all times, especially if the table responds, so don't break the bond by running in small circles if something exciting happens.

It's okay if nothing happens the first few times. You'll get into the ghost groove with more practice, so keep trying!

DOWSiNG RODS

How can two metal rods help find ghosts? Used for centuries as tools to discover underground water sources, dowsing rods (or divining rods) can wiggle their way into the paranormal spectrum by picking

While it's never been proven that table tipping has anything to do with actual ghosts, it is commonly believed that the combination of subconscious human minds working together may explain the rappings and actual movement of the table. How? No one's been able to explain that one either...

up on *electromagnetic fields,* much like your compass and a pendulum.

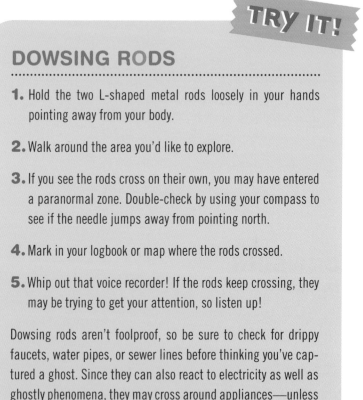

TRY IT!

DOWSING RODS

1. Hold the two L-shaped metal rods loosely in your hands pointing away from your body.

2. Walk around the area you'd like to explore.

3. If you see the rods cross on their own, you may have entered a paranormal zone. Double-check by using your compass to see if the needle jumps away from pointing north.

4. Mark in your logbook or map where the rods crossed.

5. Whip out that voice recorder! If the rods keep crossing, they may be trying to get your attention, so listen up!

Dowsing rods aren't foolproof, so be sure to check for drippy faucets, water pipes, or sewer lines before thinking you've captured a ghost. Since they can also react to electricity as well as ghostly phenomena, they may cross around appliances—unless you think your toaster has started sending you messages from beyond, always remember to do a double-check.

LiGHT AS A FEATHER, STiFF AS A BOARD

Make your own floating head (or body) with this simple game that defies explanation.

TRY IT!

LIGHT AS A FEATHER, STIFF AS A BOARD

....

1. Have one person lie on the floor while the rest of your guests surround her, each slipping two fingers beneath the body.

2. Starting with the guest at the head, begin a story of how your poor friend met her untimely demise, and have each guest add to the tale until you complete the circle.

3. Have each girl repeat one part of the chant:

"She doesn't look well."

"She's looking worse."

"Dibs on her boyfriend." (Just wanted to see if you were paying attention!)

"She's almost dead."

"She's a goner."

4. As you begin to lift the body, have all participants (except the body, she can't move unless she's a zombie) repeat, "Light as a feather, stiff as a board," until she feels weightless and is lifted off the floor.

This may take a little practice, so don't give up if your friend isn't bumping into the ceiling on the first try.

PENDULUM

Who would have thought that a sassy accessory like a necklace or charm bracelet would be a handy way to chat up ghosts? Pendulums have been used as simple tools for finding water and locating lost objects, but you can also use them for answering questions and tracking ghosts on your investigations.

A pendulum is made up of a length of chain or ribbon with a weight at the end, such as pendant or heavy bead. Watching the weight swing in certain directions can help you determine if it's giving you the high sign on ghost phenomena.

PENDULUM

1. Rest your elbow on a steady surface and get comfy. Hold the chain between your thumb and forefinger or middle finger. Make sure the chain is long enough to swing freely but not drag on the table. Before you begin, make sure the chain is as steady as possible so you don't influence the movement of the pendant or bob.

2. Determine how you would like to receive your answers. Back and forth for yes and side to side for no? Or going in circles, either clockwise or counterclockwise? If you can't decide, ask the pendulum to give you a heads-up and show you what it prefers.

3. After you've got down the yes and no, ask it a simple question like, "Is it Tuesday?" or, "Am I wearing shoes?" At first, you may not get any response, but keep trying until you see that bad boy start swinging.

4. Once you've got the hang of it, try asking questions that require a little more finesse by using the circular alphabet below. Hold the pendulum over the center dot, and ask if your phantom guide can spell out a name or answer a question by gently swinging over each letter. Have a friend record the letters so you don't break your ghost mojo. This will take a little practice, so don't worry if it comes out jumbled at first.

USE YOUR PENDULUM
ON A GHOST HUNT

f you suspect paranormal activity in a room, pull out your
pendulum, and begin asking questions. If you are in a larger
location and have a map, hold the pendulum over the area you
want to explore, and the bob should swing toward where it feels you
will find the strongest evidence of ghosts.

BLOODY MARY

"Bloody Mary, Bloody Mary, Bloody Mary!" Simple tongue twister or more insidious? The Bloody Mary legend has its roots tangled in history. Is she the ghost of Mary Tudor, the English queen who had her people tortured and killed in the name of religion? Or perhaps she is Mary Worth, a witch who found herself at the wrong end of a match over a hundred years ago but now seeks revenge?

TRY IT!

BLOODY MARY

1. Choose a room that can become completely dark, such as a bathroom, and shut the door.

2. Turn off the light, and stand to face the mirror.

3. Chant "Bloody Mary" three times without blinking.

4. Turn on the light while facing the mirror to see if Mary has indeed come to visit you!

RECIPE

BLOODY MUDDY GHOST COOKIES

Ingredients:

* Two soft and gooey chocolate chip cookies
* Marshmallow fluff
* Sliced strawberries
* Chocolate bar

This recipe makes a perfect snack for after a ghost hunt or hanging out with friends. Layer marshmallow fluff, straw-berries, and bits of the chocolate bar between two chocolate chip cookies. Pop it into the microwave for 15 seconds, remove (carefully, it will be hot), and munch!

TOP TEN FAVORITE GHOST FLICKS

Put a little fright in your night with one of these great ghost flicks. You can't go wrong with our Bloody Muddy Ghost Cookies, dim lights, and a friend to scare the socks off of at the spooky parts.

Ghostbusters (1984, Rated PG): Sharp, funny, and a total classic. If this doesn't have you strapping on your proton pack by the time the credits roll, read *The Girls' Ghost Hunting Guide* again, my friend.

Poltergeist (1982, Rated PG): This film gave the nation a twitch every time a television went a little fuzzy and *really* gave clowns a bad name. The perfect scary movie, but don't watch it alone!

Haunted Mansion (2003, Rated PG): Gracey Manor is up for sale, but who will be the 1,000th ghost to move in?

The Haunting (1963, Not rated): From Shirley Jackson's *The Haunting of Hill House*, *The Haunting* is terrifying without being gory. When a parapsychologist tests the powers of Hill House and invites others in for the weekend, the house reacts…badly. But is it the ghosts of the children trapped within its walls or the house itself that drives Eleanor Lance mad?

The Sixth Sense (1999, Rated PG-13): After failing to help a former client, child psychologist Malcolm Crowe wants to make amends by focusing his attention on Cole, who sees dead people. While his own life falls apart, Crowe helps Cole to live with his abilities, but at what cost?

Beetlejuice (1988, Rated PG): So what's a nice dead couple to do when a terrible family moves into their house? When their attempts to scare them away fail, the Maitlands enlist the help of bio-exorcist Beetlejuice. And you thought the creepy uncle living in your basement was hard to get rid of!

Lady in White (1988, Rated PG-13): Witnessing the murder of a young girl at his school, a boy can't escape the feeling that he knows the killer while being drawn to a spooky old house. Does the Lady in White hold the key to the mystery?

Nancy Drew (2007, Rated PG): Everyone's favorite girl detective moves to sunny California, and with the help of a ghost, unravels the murder mystery of a movie star.

Coraline (2009, Rated PG): After Coraline moves to the state of Oregon, she finds the house her family now lives in has a sinister history. Curious and bored, she scratches the surface to discover another dimension where everything she wants is hers for the asking—but is there a darker purpose to the Other Mother's generosity?

Blackbeard's Ghost (1968, Not rated): Cursed to roam forever until he does a good deed, can Blackbeard the pirate give up his scallywag ways to help a group of ladies keep their home?

FEARLESS PHANTOM GAME

Ghosts and goblins aren't just for Halloween anymore! Start a year-round tradition of booing your friends with the Fearless Phantom game. As the sun sets, place baskets of spooky fun on the doorsteps of your friends and neighbors, ring the doorbell, and run back to your house. Include our poem and a copy of this ghost in the basket.

It all started with a little BOO.
A knock upon the door and off he flew!

The Phantom was here.
He left a tiny friend.

Put him in your window
So the fun never ends.

The Fearless Phantom has struck! It's your turn to send the Phantom on his way with ghostly goodies. Be sure to copy or draw your own Phantom so he can wave to your friends!

Basket ideas:

* CREEPY DVDS   * PUZZLES
* CANDY   * GHOST STORIES
* GAMES

QUESTION FROM A FUTURE GHOST HUNTER

WHAT IS THE WEIRDEST THING YOU'VE EVER SEEN AS A GHOST HUNTER?
Breanna W., age 11

During one investigation, the lead investigator asked me to sit in a child's room that was reported to be haunted. Holding a doll, I sat in the darkened room alone and felt a chill come over me. A large, cold spot hovered near me to see the "baby." We felt this was the same old woman's spirit that had been heard doing the nightly dishes, then slowly clomping up the stairs with her cane. The cold spot stayed for a very long time, then slowly moved away, and I could finally release that breath I'd been holding. Phew!

I'm still a bit freaked out about shadow people, to be honest. I didn't start seeing them in investigations until 2010, while at an alleged haunted home on the fringe of the Bull Run battlefield in Manassas, Virginia. After seeing a black figure move along the exposed upstairs hallway and move into a bedroom, I knew the house wasn't as quiet on the inside as it seemed on the outside. Later that year, I noticed shadow people in my own house…

CHAPTER 4

Haunted Objects

WHAT CREATES A HAUNTED object? What saturates something that has no soul so that it carries with it the pain of a broken heart or the violence of a death? Call it cursed, call it blessed—these items frequently bump into our lives, creating phenomena that can't be explained by blaming the cat. Haunted cribs, chairs that doom people to horrible deaths, or dolls that you thought only existed in bad movies—the mundane creates its own horror through the memories forced on it by former owners and passed on to new ones. You may think twice before hitting the next garage sale.

I have a friend that collects haunted things; it's become an obsession for him. He travels to New Orleans and brings back authentic voodoo dolls for my children. He gave one of these dolls to a lady who put it away in a cupboard so it wouldn't tempt the cats as a plaything. That same night, she developed a headache and went to lie down on the couch. Upon her awakening a few hours later, the doll was sitting on the table next to her head. Since returning it to the cupboard, she periodically hears scratching coming from the cabinet. I'd be setting very large mousetraps just in case!

Another item that has developed a wandering streak is a clown doll bought at auction; it has gone missing for weeks only to turn up again on a bookshelf. It seems small, cheerful, and harmless, but we wonder if it has anything to do with the television as well—the TV changes channels whenever the clown is sitting atop it. Since the clown has entered the picture, my friend has been subjected to phantom knockings at the door—ones that are only a few feet off the ground.

Can haunted objects be passed down to others? Just ask anyone living in a haunted house.

Muncaster Castle, Great Britain

The lion doesn't necessarily sleep at night in this centuries-old castle in the Lake District of England. The ghost of the great cat prowls the darkened hallways after its skull was brought to the castle by the last Lord Muncaster from his safari in Kenya. It joins the spirit of a young girl, Margaret Susan Pennington, a family ancestor who died of screaming fits in the nineteenth century in the now reportedly haunted Tapestry Room. The room hosts other ghostly phenomena such as footsteps, doors opening and shutting by themselves, and guests feeling as if they were being watched, or being subjected to a surprise concert by a singing woman. Known now to be a former children's nursery, the Tapestry Room continues to be the center of Muncaster's hauntings and is regularly visited by paranormal investigators.

One of Muncaster Castle's more nefarious ghosts is Tom Skelton, known as Tom Fool, the last court jester in England's long history, who died near the end of the sixteenth century. The legend states that he would send those looking for the way to the castle into the quicksand and boggy marsh near the River Esk while he rested under a favorite chestnut tree. Some made it through the treacherous terrain to the castle, while others did not. He is considered to be responsible for the murder of a carpenter in love with Sir Ferdinand Pennington's daughter, Helwise. The carpenter has been seen carrying his head tucked under his arm; he's apparently still looking for some*body* to love.

Mary Bragg haunts the castle as the Muncaster Boggle (ghost). Murdered by thugs hired by a romantic rival while she worked as a housekeeper in the castle, Mary's body was found floating in the River Esk, though the cause of death is not clear due to the horrific state her body was found in—eels had nibbled off her face. Her ghost is a vision wrapped in white seen on the grounds of Muncaster and surrounding roads, sometimes leaping in front of cars before vanishing.

PSYCHOMETRY

Let's take your psychic skills for a test drive! Some people are able to learn about the history of objects such as jewelry, eyeglasses, or clothing through touch. Psychics use this skill to help investigators discover more about a case through the material objects left behind. Want to discover what's behind the mystery of that old ring?

TRY IT!

PSYCHOMETRY

1. Hold an object lightly in your hands and relax.

2. Concentrate and allow your mind to receive messages that may come to you through touching the object. You're using your senses to interpret its history, so look for certain smells, tastes, sounds, feelings, or mental visions that pop up.

3. The first images are usually the strongest. Have a friend record what you say while describing your feelings so you can interpret them later.

Black Aggie

The dark stare of a hooded woman wrapped in a shroud of sorrow and pain watched over the body of General Felix Agnus in the early twentieth century. The monument, nearly a direct copy of a statue from the famous Adams Memorial in Washington, D.C., known by the name of *Grief*, rested not far from its doppelganger at the Druid Ridge Cemetery in Pikesville, Maryland. In the sunlight, Black Aggie was a magnificent work of art, but as night fell, stories swept across the area about the woman whose eyes glowed red at midnight and spirits from the graveyard gathered around her in homage. Pregnant women were reported to have miscarried their children if they passed too close to where her shadow fell on bare land. Grass never grew around the monument, and those who dared to look into her gaze were blinded.

The legend grew, sparking the imagination of a local fraternity. Part of their initiation rite for new members was to have the young men crouch beneath the statue with their backs to the graves. One night, a watchman responded to a cry for help from two fraternity brothers and found a boy lying dead at the monument's feet. The brothers told him they had seen Black Aggie's eyes glow and her arms reach out to crush her victim. When she sought them as well, they ran away, terrified.

The public became fascinated with the story and visited Aggie to see if they, too, could get the statue to move. Eventually, the cemetery had it removed, and it found a home with the National Museum of American Art. It remained in storage for years until finding a home in the rear courtyard of the Dolley Madison House at the Federal Courts Building in Washington, D.C., where you may visit her today.

TOMBSTONE SYMBOLS

What can a tombstone tell you about the person beneath your feet? Some stones have only the name and dates of birth and death, while others can give a glimpse of the person's life: if they were married, died at sea, a cherished husband or an innocent child. The use of symbols on the stones can help fill in the blanks regarding a full—or very short—life.

* **ANCHOR:** sailors, sea death, hope for a better tomorrow

* **ANGEL:** guide to Heaven

* **BEEHIVE:** home and education

* **BIRDS:** peace

* **BONES OR A SKELETON:** death

* **BROKEN FLOWER OR BUD:** the death was premature, or the person was very young

* **BUTTERFLY:** resurrection

* **CIRCLE:** everlasting life

* **COLUMN:** the separation of life and death

* **CROSS:** Christian faith

* **DAISY:** innocence; the daisy is usually found with young children

* **DRAGON:** chaos

* **FLAME OR TORCH:** eternity; if the torch is upside down, it means the extinguishing of life

* **HAND POINTING DOWN:** hand of God descending from Heaven

* **HAND POINTING UP:** pointing to Heaven

* **HANDSHAKE:** unity and friendship

* **HORSE:** symbol of death, a white horse stands for goodness, while a black horse depicts evil

* **IVY:** friendship

* **KNOT:** marriage and unity

* **LAMB:** innocence; usually found atop a child's tombstone

* **LAMP:** wisdom

* **LION:** strength

* **LOTUS:** rebirth and resurrection

* **MAN WITH AN HOURGLASS OR SICKLE:** Father Time or Death

* **MOON:** rebirth and resurrection

* **OWL:** wisdom

* **POPPIES:** eternal sleep

* **RABBIT:** gentleness, humility

* **SHELL:** rebirth and resurrection

* **SHOES:** commonly found with the loss of a child, one shoe may be overturned

* **SKULL:** death and mortality

* **SKULL AND CROSSBONES:** death and mortality

* **SOLDIER ON A HORSE:** with two or more hooves raised, the soldier died during battle; with one hoof off the ground, the soldier died from battle wounds. Four hooves on the ground meant the soldier died of natural causes.

* **SUN:** soul rising to Heaven

* **THISTLE:** earthly sorrow

* **TREE TRUNK OR STUMP:** a life cut short

* **TULIP:** love, for even after a tulip is cut it keeps growing

* **URN:** the soul

* **URN WITH BLAZING FIRE:** undying friendship

* **WEEPING WILLOW:** sorrow

* **WEEPING WOMAN:** sorrow

* **WOMAN HOLDING AN ANCHOR:** hope

* **WREATH:** victory in death

R.I.P.

Women in Ghost Hunting: Bev Sninchak

ORGANIZATION: Colorado Springs Paranormal Association (CSPA)

WEBSITE: www.paranormalcoloradosprings.org *or* www.cspa.co

YEARS AS A GHOST INVESTIGATOR: 7 years

Nocturnal by nature, I am is a published author, editor, and writing coach. After experiencing unexplained phenomena following the death of my first husband and then capturing my first EVP in January 2005, I decided to dedicate my life to investigating paranormal phenomena. My specific interests include quantum physics and EVP.

The Colorado Springs Paranormal Association (CSPA) conducts investigations and research into claims of supernatural phenomena primarily through the use of scientific methods supplemented by intuitive means. Our research tools include—but may not be limited to—the use of photography, audio/video recordings, environmental monitors, and intuitive researchers. We prefer to approach things from a scientific, rational approach. We look for mundane explanations first and foremost, and then deal with what's leftover that we can't explain. Some of us believe quantum physics may explain instances of paranormal activity.

Some of our video evidence was recently featured on the Season Two finale of the Biography Channel's *My Ghost Story* (which aired June 11, 2011).

GGHG *What is your background with the paranormal? Did it start at an early age or as an adult?*

BS: I first began reading about and studying the paranormal when I was a preteen, about nine or ten years old. I would go to the library after school and immerse myself in the occult section. I can't remember a time when I wasn't interested in the paranormal or the unexplained.

GGHG *What happened on your first formal investigation? Floating heads or a quiet night?*

BS: It was fairly quiet the first time out. Later on, once we went over the data, we captured the voice of a Southern lady who was rambling on about the table for some reason—it didn't make sense, but we never expected to get that voice! On a follow-up investigation, I was sitting in a chair in a corner with a vacuum cleaner stored in that corner, and out of the blue, the vacuum cleaner was picked up and dropped down force-fully with a loud *crash!* There was nobody or nothing with that corner, and another investiga-tor sitting by me saw the thing lift up and get dropped back down to the floor!

GGHG *Do you use the help of mediums during your investigations?*

BS: No, we do not. We have found that if you use psychics or mediums, then people glom on to only what they say (which may be true, but there's usually no concrete proof to the stories that are being told), and the clients then do not listen to the information we are giving them or the audio/video evidence we are attempting to present to them. So we decided we would not utilize that type of resource.

CHAPTER 5

Making the Dead Speak

WE'VE ALL BEEN THERE, huddled under a sleeping bag with marshmallows stuck in our hair while reading or listening to a great ghost story. What? No marshmallows? You don't know what you're missing. The storyteller spins her tale of brokenhearted ghosts and eyeless phantoms, of untimely deaths and the scrapes of hooks against car doors. Falling asleep isn't easy, but the scarier the plot, the more we believe, just for a second, that those shadows fading into the night may be looking for us, and the shivers running down our spines are the bony fingers of doom.

HOW TO WRITE A GREAT GHOST STORY

Writing your own ghost story is a piece of cake with these easy steps:

Whose pants are you trying to scare off? Younger kids generally need less gore and more lore when telling a story. While it's fine to hint at dark deeds, it may be better to blame that weird smell on the dog (if you get my drift) rather than the bodies stacked under the bed.

For older friends, spin a story about a common fear: death, abandonment, cafeteria food, strangers, or even what happens at night to all that gum that's stuck under the science desks. The gum you were smackin' may be the one they are snackin' on later.

Suspense sticks with a reader long after the gooey bits have dried up. Plant a seed of what's going to come in the first few chapters of your story (foreshadowing), so your readers will have that "*aha!*" moment when the climax happens. In the beginning of your story, mention that your heroine hates rats. You know later she'll have a rodent crawl in her ear to lay baby rats in her brain, only to have them eat her gray matter and crawl out her nose. Okay, I've just grossed myself out. I need a minute.

Choose the right scary character for the right job. The neighbor down the street who waters his lawn while wearing a tutu is a lot more frightening than what you'll see in the movies. As you build your characters, think about some of the more *interesting* quirks you've noticed in the people around you. Adding familiar mannerisms to your ghost makes it more real for the reader or listener—and more frightening. That lovely cat lady down the street? What do you think is in her pets' cat chow, and when was the last time you saw your little brother?

Great ghost stories involve characters that have a back story before you begin to write. It will make it easier to remember why your characters do what they do. It doesn't have to be super involved— just jot down what they're afraid of and how they got that way. There may be an evil secret holding a boy back from going into the graveyard at night with his friends. Is he afraid he'll be pulled back into his grave? Does the girl avoid the water because she's afraid of shampoo in her eyes or because she's dreamed about spirits staring up at her from the cold blue-green depths of the sea?

Sleepovers and campouts are a perfect time for creating a story with your friends. Before you go to bed, have everyone take a turn telling part of your ghost tale, with one person writing it all down to share later in an email.

Put a little boogie in your boo. All stories need rhythm, a cadence that moves them along and keeps the reader interested. What problem does your main character need to solve before the end of the story? She starts the tale happy, then she's terrified, then she's solved one problem (happy), only to be plunged back into the pits (oooh, bad). Your job is to get your readers back to a happy place—or better yet, completely freaked out and calling their mom. (Success!)

Was it a dark and stormy night? Atmosphere and location set the mood, but don't limit yourself to only haunted houses or cobweb-covered graveyards. Hauntings happen during daylight hours as well. How about a full-bodied apparition appearing on a busy sidewalk or riding the bus? Don't limit yourself to what's already familiar in your favorite books; create an unexpected spot for your story to unfold. I bet you'll surprise yourself.

Weave your story world by using your senses to show what your hero is experiencing. What is she tasting or smelling? Can she feel the coldness as the ghost

Writing ideas on index cards are a great way to mobilize your story. You're able to cluster characters and the horrible things that happen to them in piles, then rearrange as you see the story fit together. Having the information at your fingertips instead of crowded notes helps you to sort out what the best bits are and leave other ideas to the side for future stories.

passes through her? Does your ghost crave donuts? By filling in the holes, you're making a good story awesome and having more fun in the process.

So, what the heck happens? You introduced your characters, set the atmosphere, and know that something really, really bad is going to happen to the poor kid. The *plot* is made up of the juicy bits of the story that show how your characters get into a mess, then out of it. Here is where you keep the action going and move your story forward, so it doesn't lie there twitching on the side of the road. A strong plot keeps readers interested, while a weaker one leaves them rooting around the refrigerator for leftover cheese sticks—don't be a cheese stick.

Plot development puts the *scare* in *scaredy-pants*. Let your imagination go nutty, and see what deserted, tangled path it leads you down.

Lay the dead back down to rest. Ghost stories often end with a lingering dread of what's hiding under the bed or a last-minute fright fest that leaves your reader screaming and sleeping with the light on. Do you want to end your story with wild-eyed readers or keep them thinking about what could happen if they just took one little bite of Phantom Pudding?

Putting It All Together

Now that you have a rough idea of how you want your story to develop, it's time to make an outline. Stop groaning. Your English teacher was actually right on this. An outline will help you to organize those crazy ideas you have floating around on sticky notes or in your head.

EXAMPLE!

CHARACTERS: Poppy (main character), Mellie (best friend), Carole (best friend), Aly (best friend)

SETTING: Mellie's house for a sleepover

PLOT: The girls have told Poppy that they've seen her trapped within a mirror that Mellie's mother picked up at an antiques store. They've dared her to face the mirror alone in the dark.

PROBLEM: Poppy's afraid to look in the mirror, though she knows it's just a silly story.

ACTION: Poppy faces the mirror and her fears.

ATMOSPHERE: Fun sleepover with friends turns scary. Dark room, unfamiliar house, queasy from too much pizza.

CONCLUSION: Poppy turns to face the glass, then sees herself within the mirror, banging against the frame with her fists and screaming. She turns to run from the room and finds herself trapped in the frame while her mirror image turns, smiles, and goes downstairs to her friends after telling Poppy to hush with a grin and a raised finger to her lips.

After you have organized your notes, have some fun with the first draft. Get creative, and let your imagination spill out onto the page. There's no limit on words—when the story is finished, stop. When you're happy with it, let it sit for a week or so—no peeking—then go back and look at the story with fresh eyes. Clean up the spelling errors, make it sparkle, and share it with your friends. You're an author!

A great free program to download with your parents' permission is FreeMind (freemind.sourceforge.net/wiki/index.php/Main_Page). It's a simple mind-mapping application that creates an outline in either bubble or tree form to help sort out your story.

FiNiSH THE STORY

ehind the quiet drip of rain outside her window, Sinjin heard the smallest of noises—a faint tapping within her room. Her eyes snapping open, she lurched forward into a sitting position on the bed, her hands wide as if warding off an unseen attacker. Scanning the unfamiliar room, she saw nothing amiss. The room was large and comfortable, with heavy dark furniture and an old-fashioned fan wobbling above her head, stirring the morning's humid air. Turning her head slightly, she listened again for the noise and was met with only silence.

"I'm losing my mind, and it's not even breakfast yet," she grumbled.

How would you finish the story? What made that noise, and how did Sinjin end up in a strange room? What or who will she discover when she goes downstairs for breakfast?

What would you do? Finish the story on the lines below, and share with your friends. What would they do differently?

knew I shouldn't have listened to Peter. He's always getting me into trouble." Elizabeth pulled her sweater tighter around her thin body, trying to mold the pattern into her skin in a vain attempt to make it warmer. Spending the night in a graveyard was ridiculous, she knew, but Jake had a way of making things sound reasonable. Like sleeping at the feet of Black Aggie…

"I bet he doesn't even show up," she muttered. Alone in the graveyard, she still didn't feel comfortable speaking out loud—why taunt the dead when you didn't have to? Her eyes swept the quiet meadow littered with monuments and head-stones in various states of decay, but she refused to look up at the one hovering over her. Black Aggie had a reputation for coming alive on dark nights and pulling those who dared to be near her down to the underworld. Elizabeth was going to prove to Jake that she wasn't afraid of an urban legend and could spend the night comfortably alone with whatever spooks and goblins he thought might visit.

Her Chucks poking at a shard of a broken soda bottle sticking up from the ground near Black Aggie's barren patch of lawn, she thought about the others who had dared to spend the night in the path of the monument's dead-eyed stare. Had they finished the task? Or had their luck run out? Clouds blocked the last of the starlight, and as her eyes adjusted to the new level of darkness, she felt the cold once more seeping into her bones.

"This is stupid; there's no way I'm catching pneumonia to sit out here for a statue." Finally daring to turn to look Black Aggie in the eyes, she felt her breath being torn from her lungs, her feet rooted to the ground…

What happens next to Elizabeth and Black Aggie? Finish the story on the lines below.

....

....

....

....

....

....

....

....

....

....

GETTING THE ZOMBIES OUT OF THE CHEESE DIP: HOW TO TELL A GREAT GHOST STORY

The moon was high overhead; light trickled through the bare branches and played around the tents that dotted the forest floor. Circling a small fire sat seven children, each only a breath away from the darkness that lay outside the warmth of the fire pit. One girl, the oldest, spoke softly. Her hands fluttered wildly, soundless participants to back up the words of the horror she told to her small audience. As their eyes grew wide, the children huddled closer together to catch her last breathy sentence, and she suddenly threw back her head and yelled to the stars, "*Gotcha!*" Last thing we knew, those children were still running…!

You learned how to write a ghost story in the previous section. Now, let's go over the steps to really make your sleepover scary.

Have a partner: A secret partner helps set the mood. Make sure your partner is seated farthest away during the story so all eyes are on you. Have her ask a question if the story strays that will bring your listeners back to attention. When the time is right, have your partner grab the person next to her for effect.

Tell the story: Speak softly so the audience will need to lean in to hear you. This demands listeners' concentration so the focus won't be on your partner. Use hand gestures to tell the story. The more animated you become, the more involved they will be themselves. Pace yourself so the telling doesn't come out in a rush, putting the zombies in the cheese dip before the marshmallows are ready to eat.

Keep the story short and punchy. You want to leave an impression, not put them to sleep. Add suspense with details: a hook, a missing eyeball, a suspicious limp caused by a leg slowly turning to goo.

Create atmosphere: Plan your story before your friends arrive. Practice with your partner to determine where the good bits are and where you need a little zing. By adding some decorations to your house pre-party, you can spice up the atmosphere with ghost goodies. Someone lose a finger in your story? Have a few fake fingers poking out of air vents. Don't make your props too obvious—you'll want your guests to find them after you're done with the tales o' gore.

Wrap it up: Every good story needs a satisfactory ending. With a ghost story, you're looking for a physical reaction to what you've told your listeners—a scream, a jump, or a quick dialing of parents on the cell phone. The last bit should drag out slowly; create suspense by speaking softly and intently. For safety reasons, your partner should be prepared to grab a person who is *not* holding a flaming marshmallow on a stick. At the climax of your story, end with a bang, not a shrug, and watch them dig for bugs with their shoes. Crafting the perfect ghost story takes imagination, preparation, and a great sense of humor. Relax, have fun, and save me a marshmallow!

Glamis Castle

Secret rooms, bloodstained stones, and pacts with the Devil have shrouded Scotland's Glamis Castle in mystery and hauntings. Shakespeare's Macbeth is rumored to have murdered King Duncan within its walls, and Malcolm II's bloody death stained the floor so violently that the room was bricked up. Did the echoes of these events leave a residue that walks at night?

Glamis's brutal history may have started with a card game. One legend tells of the second lord of Glamis, in the fifteenth century, who was well known for a corrupt lifestyle. Famous for gambling and drinking, he earned the nickname "Earl Beardie" or "the Wicked Lord." One Sunday evening, after failing to find someone to play cards with him, he announced that he would play with the Devil himself. The knock on the door immediately afterward was too much of a coincidence, but he opened it anyway to find a tall, bearded man wearing all black.

When asked if he would still like a partner to play cards with, Earl Beardie welcomed the man into a small secret room and closed the door. Servants outside could hear shouting and furniture flying as the men gambled away the evening and into the dark night. At one point, the stranger made a suggestion to which Earl Beardie agreed. One of the servants crept close to the door to see what was happening through the keyhole, at which point the lord discovered he was being spied upon. He burst from the room to yell at the servant, but when he returned, the stranger had left and taken Earl Beardie's soul with him. Beardie died five years later, but his ghost still drunkenly roams the halls. Trapped for eternity, he continuously returns to the room to play cards with the Devil.

Other rooms taunt the curious as well. During the eighteenth century, a legend started saying that a room held secrets so horrible that only the Earl of Strathmore, his heir, and the steward of the castle were allowed to view it. As the lords reached their twenty-first birthdays, some chose not to enter the room for fear of what was inside. The most popular theory today is that the room held the remains of a rightful heir born deformed and locked away. Rumors of ghosts swirled around the castle to distract the curious from the truth. In order to find that hidden room, towels were once hung in every window of the castle, yet if viewed from outside, there was one room without. To this day, no amount of searching has produced an entrance from within the castle to that secret room.

Glamis has its own white or gray lady. She is believed to be the ghost of Janet Douglas, the wife of the sixth Lord of Glamis, James. After his death, she was suspected of killing him, but in the absence of evidence, the charges were dropped. However, Douglas had gained the reputation of being a witch. There was no evidence needed for a trial of that kind, so when she came under suspicion for plotting the murder of the King of Scotland, she was tried, condemned, and executed in Edinburgh in 1537. Her ghost returned home and now wanders the halls of Glamis, looking for justice.

QUESTION FROM A FUTURE GHOST HUNTER

HOW DO YOU GET STARTED AS A GHOST HUNTER?
Breanna W., age 11

Excellent question! To get started, you need great research skills to get the skinny on the location, an open mind—but not so open that your brain falls out and you believe anything you see or hear—and curiosity. It's that curious streak that keeps tickling our imaginations, making us want to learn more about what's on the other side.

You don't need a lot of fancy equipment; the simplest way to begin is to pay attention to your senses while you're investigating. What you feel, hear, and see is the most important part of any ghost hunt; all the other ghost-hunting goodies can wait. It's also important to keep good notes. And remember, don't automatically assume everything is a sign from beyond. A mouse in the walls can sound an awful lot like paranormal scratchings in the middle of the night, so think of what else could make that noise before proclaiming it a ghost.

CHAPTER 6

Investigation Boogie, Part 1

BEFORE YOU HEAD OUT the door for your investigation, go over the following sections to be prepared for what comes next. Research and information are your best tools when you leap into the murky world of the paranormal, so be sure to keep your notes together and communicate with the rest of your team for the best experience.

PUTTING YOUR INVESTIGATIVE TEAM TOGETHER

It's not safe to hunt ghosts alone. Who's going to go with you on your new adventure? Investigations run best if the jobs are divided up among team members. Then everyone plays an equal part, and no one feels left out or overwhelmed with too many responsibilities. Here are some of the jobs that can be divvied up.

Lead Investigator: Are you the one with the great ideas who knows how to put a party together in a moment's notice? The Lead Investigator (or LI) has natural leadership abilities but knows when to share the spotlight and have fun. The LI will be the girl who has a brilliant idea at bedtime and has designed business cards and a website for the group before breakfast.

The LI will also be the group's main contact for the area or house you'll be investigating as well as be in charge of dividing the group into teams. All team members should report their findings back to her following the investigation.

After the team members have gathered information and come to a conclusion about what they've seen, heard, or smelled, the LI presents the conclusion back to the homeowner.

Researcher: Responsible for gathering as much background information as possible on locations, the Researcher helps the group piece together possible explanations for what's going on, as well as creating a time line of past homeowners or area history. Is the problem a sewer line gone bad (ew) or has the house been built over an ancient Indian burial ground, making someone very, very cranky?

Every team member needs to know the background of the location to be investigated. The Researcher gives them a heads-up before they go out so no one is left in the dark.

Photographer: Have a great eye for detail? The Photographer position may be for you!

The Photographer is responsible for videotaping the homeowner interviews. She makes sure the equipment is in working order and that the interviews are recorded, not mysteriously blank by the end of the night.

Interviewer: Being able to chat someone's head off is one of the most valuable jobs in the group. If you're ready to really get the scoop on a haunting, the Interviewer is the girl that can put people at ease and help them to remember pieces of the puzzle that may have been missing. Check the Interview section for sample questions so you'll hit the ground running when ghosts pop up.

EVP Specialist: While EVPs are fun to do, it helps to have someone keep track of all the mumbling and dead silence in one place. The EVP Specialist will gather the files at the end of the investigation and go over them again and again. She will try to sort through which noises could be the whispers of the team about what to put on the pizza later and what could be an actual paranormal event. She'll be the one responsible for writing down what was heard—if anything—and sharing it with the group later. Check out the section on how to take EVP readings in better detail so your team will have the most fun with this great investigative tool.

Equipment Specialist: That's a fancy name for the person who makes sure the kits are packed properly and everyone has extra batteries. She's the peanut butter that keeps this sandwich stuck together! She'll see that everyone has their dowsing rods and cell phones charged, that extra water and snacks are tucked away for later, and that each team member is ready to roll.

Skeptic: Have someone in the group that doesn't believe in ghosts but is willing to learn something new? Perfect! As we know, a healthy percentage of hauntings turn out to have simple explanations rather than paranormal ones, so having a girl with an open mind and her feet on the ground is very valuable. While it's a drag to keep hearing "That's nothing but the wind," or, "I saw the car's headlights bounce off that guy's bald head, it's not an orb," her input can keep the group grounded enough to look for scientific evidence when others are running around in small circles.

Adult: Each group should have at least one of these handy people around. An adult may be able to offer reasonable explanations for activity that you can follow up on later, as well as being someone to make sure the dark room you're investigating is mouse-free.

A great resource to bounce ideas off, an adult can offer you the added benefit of transportation. Trust me, carrying your ghost hunting kit on the bus can get a little hairy.

Clients may also be more at ease when an adult is present, so take advantage of their curiosity, and ask them to come (they'll probably be tagging along in the background anyway).

Other adults who can help are professionals such as plumbers, construction workers, electrical pros, police officers, and teachers. Each can contribute to your investigation with fresh ideas, leads, and practical knowledge of houses that can help find the source of your haunting.

NOWHERE TO RUN TO, BABY, NOWHERE TO HIDE: WHERE TO FIND GHOSTS

Ghosts may be found almost anywhere, but these places are perfect to start your research into the unknown. Choose your location.

Hotels: They always eat the corn nuts in your hotel room! Guests check in—but they don't always check out. Hotels are a great place for investigations if you give them a (floating) heads-up that you're there for the ghosties. It's thought that people leave residual energy wherever they go, but what happens if the hotel is the last place they visit? Make sure you have permission from the hotel staff before wandering around the halls at night, or the scariest guest you see may be the businessman down the hall yelling at you while trying to get some sleep. Remember to respect your fellow hotel guests, be responsible, and always leave a tip for your ghostly housekeeper.

Schools: These kids don't go home for summer vacation... There's a lot of ghostly energy roaming the halls of schools as the spirits of children and college-aged kids reportedly return to be around old friends. Some teachers are a little too attached to their classrooms as well—may be waiting for that book report you promised them.

If you want to find out more about your school's history, check with the front office or teachers who have been teaching at the school for a while. They may have some stories to tell about what's *really* in the Friday meatloaf.

Battlefields: And the rockets' red glare... Sure, they're quiet now, but while the troops battled each other over a strip of land, it was a hotbed of drama.

What's often left behind is a residue of emotion, fear, anger, and sadness imprinted on the area.

Theaters: Some people just don't know when to exit, stage left. Ever daydream about being onstage or in the movies? The adoration of millions, the fancy cars, or your name spelled out in Cheez Whiz? Yeah, me too. Some ghosts aren't willing to take a bow and skedaddle. They're still hanging around waiting for someone to ask for their autograph in the theaters they haunt.

Restaurants: You want fries with that? Your favorite restaurant could be serving up more than just cheeseburgers; it may have a resident ghost in the back working the lunch crowd.

Private houses: A room with a boo. Even the friendliest-looking house could have a little sumthin' sumthin' roaming around in the dark. Learn about your town's history to see if there have been reports of paranormal activity, join a local ghost tour and chat up the guide, or ask your friends if they know of a house to investigate.

FIVE FAST TIPS FROM GHOST HUNTER SUSAN UTLEY OF WEE GHOSTIES

1 The most successful ghost hunts happen when you are skeptical but still open-minded.

2 Be patient. Just because you are ready to see ghosts doesn't mean they are ready to be seen.

3 Don't be afraid to laugh. Sometimes, ghosts are funny. Sometimes, people are even more entertaining.

4 Wear comfortable shoes, and bring a sweatshirt, even in summer. Sometimes, ghosts like to hang out in chilly spots.

5 Always carry extra batteries—and don't forget to bring extra batteries.

DIGGING DEEPER: RESEARCHING THE GHOSTIES

The ghost of your research paper on the life cycle of tree frogs is coming back to haunt youuuuuu! What? Nothing? Never mind. The skills you learned finding out more about your friend the frog will help you sort through the information available on places you are investigating.

Check websites such as the Shadowlands and local newspapers for stories in your town regarding public places such as cemeteries and parks. Newspapers love to run stories around Halloween to stir up candy-happy thrill seekers. Keep in mind that these places may have strict no trespassing laws or limited access, so pay attention to their posted hours, and wrap up your ghost hunt appropriately.

If you're investigating a private home, chat up the family about what they've seen. If they're renting, see if you can contact the homeowner to get their permission too to check out the house. They may have their own stories. Ask about former owners of the place, and keep good notes on who lived there at what time. Ask questions about how long the owners have had the property and why they bought it. How long did it take to rent out (if renting)? If the house has been through a string of people, why didn't they stay longer?

So where do you find more information about a private home after you've spoken with the current non-dead residents?

Historical societies: They may have a file on strange doings at the address you'll be investigating. Get to know the historians on duty and see if they've heard anything in the past that could help identify a ghost.

Public library: It's not just a place to score a copy of the YA novel you've been dying to read. Many libraries carry books by local authors who have researched ghost stories in the area. If your branch doesn't have the information you need, talk to the librarian about other libraries in the system that can transfer books for you to check out.

No means *no!* If you come across a "No Trespassing" sign, leave the area. It's not worth getting into trouble to find out if something freaky happens when you're out at night. Aside from being private property, the area may be unsafe to roam around in, so don't take chances. There's always another ghost around the bend!

County registrar office: It holds the records of all local births, deaths, marriages, and divorces, plus real estate deals and deeds to property. For your investigation, find out who owned a house when, checking to see if anyone died in or around the house itself.

Newspaper archives: If there was a violent death associated with a house, you'll be sure the local reporters will have a story on it. Some newspapers have their archives available online for you to search.

Internet: This is an easy one. Type in an address in the search engine of your choice, and see what pops up.

Check the surrounding neighborhood as well—ghosts may not be restricted to just one house. If you know that the neighborhood itself has a history, such as being built over a battlefield or burial ground that can stir up activity, it can help you to zero in on what time period your ghosts may be from.

Church and cemetery records: As your notes come together, you may start to see the same names jump out at you over and over. If it's known what church the people belonged to, it can help to trace back how long they were part of the church community and where they were buried—or whether they were buried at all.

Nosy neighbors: That lady peeking at you through the blinds next door? She may have some juicy tidbits to share about the house. Remember that unless she was present in the home at the time it happened, however, whatever you find out from her will be hearsay and may not be reliable. Neighbors can be great resources for finding out more about the history of an area, so if they have time to chat, ask them if you can pull up a chair.

Former owners or residents: Some people will have great stories to tell about hearing footsteps or being watched, while others will not have seen a thing the entire time. Spend extra time with the kids in the house, as they often pick up on ghostly vibes a lot easier than adults. That little girl they played with in the back bedroom may not have gone home for dinner.

f there are kids in the house, pay special attention to what they have to say. Many children are able to interact with ghosts when adults can't, so if the six-year-old says she has a friend who won't share her toys in the basement, you may want to check that out.

Always check and double-check your sources and time lines. Missing notes can leave a gap for information to fall through, and you could be chasing your tail instead of ghosts. Make sure your information is as accurate as possible so you can get the best picture of who may be buried under the begonias.

INTERViEW YOUR HOSTS

An important part of any investigation is interviewing the people involved. Keep in mind that they're likely to be a bit frightened or frustrated that their home has been invaded by something that doesn't help out around the house.

Assistance can come from unexpected places, so encourage the family to participate in the process. It helps them to become less afraid of what's going bump in the night if they can focus on taking notes and recording the activity that takes place when you're not there.

When setting up a time to interview, start first by either emailing or calling. As they answer the questions, you'll be able to see if what they have is really a case to check out with your team or if you can recommend something else, such as a good plumber. For each new case, I advise that you have each homeowner start a log to record activity when you're not there for a few weeks. Ask the family to include:

* Date

* Time

* Who is in the house when it occurs

* What happened

* If it has happened before

* Any associated smells, sounds, sights, or feelings

Unfortunately, there are people that like to "test" ghost hunting groups by giving silly answers and wasting your time. Always have an adult check your ghost-related emails and never, ever meet someone alone to discuss a case. Safety first!

See the questionnaire in the appendix for samples of what to ask in your first interview. You can adjust them to each case or leave out some altogether. What else would you include?

DESIGNING YOUR TEAM LOGO

Now that you've put together a fabulous team of ghost hunters, have some fun! Design your team logo, start a blog or website, and make up some snazzy business cards on your home printer to pass out to your friends and clients.

You can have T-shirts, hats, or hoodies made with your logo to show you're the ghost hunting dream team! What's the name of your group? Do you have a slogan like, "Putting the Boo back in Boogie," or, "GHOST: Girls Having Outrageously Spooky Times." Okay, that was lame. I'm sure you'll do better.

Melanie Hooyenga, owner and lead graphic designer at Ink Slinger Designs in Michigan, gives us these pointers: Designing a logo is the perfect time to stretch your creativity. The sky's the limit—type style (font), color, dark or light—but the most important thing to remember is KISS: *Keep It Simple, Sleuths!*

Tips to keep in mind while designing your team's logo:

Small, intricate details look great on a poster. However, they are hard to see on a business card or note card. Stick to basic shapes (the outline of a spiderweb instead of one with a thousand lines), so when it prints out you'll avoid ending up with a mud puddle instead of a ghost.

The best logos have no more than one or two fonts. Check out your favorite brands for examples—the Internet is an endless supply of ideas.

DaFont.com and 1001FreeFonts.com have tons of free fonts—just be sure to get your parents' permission before downloading files from the Internet.

My favorite part: color! The only rule with color is to pick something you love. Styles and trends are always changing so there's never a wrong answer.

Happy designing!

Draw some ideas below with your friends:

YOUR GHOST HUNTiNG KiT

There's no need to spend a lot of money on ghost hunting tools; with your parents' permission, you can easily use objects around your house to get started. Packing your ghost hunting kit ahead of time is an important part of being an organized researcher, so what exactly do you need when heading out?

Paper and pen: A notebook or logbook and graph paper for mapping rooms and locations of objects are all vital to an investigation. Have a few pens or pencils handy in case one runs dry or the tip breaks.

Camera: Digital or point-and-shoot cameras are great not only to record any possible paranormal activity but also to see if items are moved or missing during the investigation. Photo-enhancing software such as Adobe Photoshop is available to adjust the contrast and shadows in your pictures so you can see if you've captured a floating head or just a really big bug.

Digital voice recorder (DVR): For recording electronic voice phenomena or taking verbal notes, a DVR is one of the tools I never leave home without when going on an investigation.

Flashlight: LED lights are lightweight and portable, and they have a much longer battery life than the old clunky ones. Each member of your team should have one, as well as a backup, in case one is lost or broken. To help keep your eyes adjusted to the dimness of a room, tape red cellophane over the lens, so it'll be easier to see. To keep your hands free, try a headband flashlight, because nothing says *awesome* like a girl with a blinding light beaming out of her forehead.

Compass: A simple hiking compass comes in handy for finding your way out of an area in case you've gotten turned around one too many times. It may also be used to chart spikes in electromagnetic fields (EMFs).

Some ghost hunters believe that EMF levels get higher when there is a ghost roaming nearby. However, you can also find high EMF readings around electrical outlets and appliances such as refrigerators and televisions, so be careful not to think your microwave is haunted!

TRY IT!

COMPASS

So that you'll get used to seeing how it works, practice with your compass outside in your backyard before going to your haunted location. First, determine where north is by watching the free-swinging (not electronic) needle point in that direction. As you move through your location, pause a few times to see if the needle swings; if it moves away from north, check to see if there are any power lines or large metal objects nearby that may interfere with EMFs, then record what time and place this happened in your logbook.

TIP: An easy way to communicate with the other side is to lay your compass on a flat surface, then ask questions if you feel there is a phantom floating around. If you see the needle jump away from north, you may be getting an answer!

Wind chimes: Hang up a small set of chimes in the areas you think may be the most haunted. Some researchers swear that the chimes alert them to a presence with a tinkle before any of their other tools pick up on the anomaly.

Watch: A timepiece is essential for keeping track of when exciting things happen, so every member of the team should have one strapped to their wrist or stuck in a pocket. There have been some reports of watches stopping during an investigation, so have an extra one handy in the group as well—just in case.

String: A small length of string can come in handy for more than tying back your hair. To check for drafts, hold it next to a window to see if it wiggles. If an object has been known to wander, wrap the string around the base to check if it has moved during your investigation.

Cell phone: Always have your emergency numbers in your contact list before heading out on an investigation. Make sure your phone is charged and ready to go!

First-aid kit: Stumbling around in dark rooms ain't for sissies. Always be alert to where you are, and have a small kit for emergencies.

An adult: Harder to get into your bag than a camera but useful just the same.

The Girls' Ghost Hunting Guide: The book in your hands is for taking notes, charting time, and writing down interview questions. Besides, I want to come too!

The best piece of equipment you can take is yourself! Trust your instincts during an investigation. If you feel like you're being watched, track back to where you think it's coming from, and take some photos or EVP readings. Use your senses to tune in to the sounds and smells around you, and don't forget to write down your impressions in your logbook to go over later.

RECIPE

POST-GHOST GRANOLA

Ingredients:

* 6 cups oats

* 3/4 cup honey

* 3/4 cup vegetable oil

* 2 teaspoons vanilla extract

* 1 tablespoon nutmeg or pumpkin pie spice

* 1 cup mini-marshmallows

* 1/2 cup M&M's or chocolate chips

* 1 cup dried fruit such as apricots, banana chips, or pineapple

Heat the oven to 300 degrees, and mix oats, honey, vegetable oil, vanilla, and nutmeg or pumpkin pie spice in a high-sided pan. Bake for 30 minutes, turning oats every ten minutes. Remove from the oven; turn the granola once more, then let cool. Mix in mini-marshmallows, M&M's or chocolate chips, and dried fruit. Take along in a zippered bag for a quick nibble on the go, have it with yogurt for breakfast the next morning, or use it as a dip for your next ice cream cone!

Mad Anthony Wayne

Revolutionary War hero and hothead Brigadier General "Mad" Anthony Wayne kicks off the New Year by searching for his bones along a lonely stretch of road in Pennsylvania. Earning his nickname from his fiery temper and bold leadership, he became a trusted part of George Washington's campaign in the Northeast against British troops in cahoots with American Indian tribes.

Dying of a particularly nasty bout of gout in December 1796, Wayne's body was buried in Fort Presque Isle, now Erie, Pennsylvania, near the foot of the flagpole, as he requested. Twelve years later, his son, Isaac Wayne, arrived to retrieve his father's body and rebury it in the family plot about 400 miles away. When the coffin was opened, the people found that Wayne's body was nearly perfectly pre-served, posing a problem regarding how to bring it home, since Isaac had only driven a small carriage and didn't want his father riding next to him. Dismembering the corpse, a doctor boiled the flesh from the bones in a kettle and then reburied what was left of Wayne, plus his clothes and the instruments used during the process, vowing never to do the procedure again.

Packing the bones in a box, Isaac left for home. As the carriage bounced down the dirt road, now Route 322, it shook the box, causing the bones to scatter along the way. Now, in the dead of winter, Mad Anthony Wayne has been reported to scour the same route his son took, looking for his bones to rejoin the flesh left at Fort Presque Isle.

Women in Ghost Hunting:
Lori Hodges

ORGANIZATION: Allegheny Paranormal
POSITION: Technical Manager/Investigator
WEBSITE: www.alleghenyparanormal.com
YEARS AS INVESTIGATOR: One year

I have seen and heard things that others didn't for as long as I can remember, ranging from random things to people actually saying my name—not just Lori, but Loretta. The only people who called me that were from my family. I've come to find out that I am apparently rather sensitive to the paranormal.

A few personal things have happened to me in places that I've lived. In the house where my parents currently live, my dad decided to replace the shower curtain with shower doors shortly after moving in. I had a friend staying the night when he replaced it. During the night, I woke up around one or two in the morning. I heard what sounded like our cat banging on the door, and shortly afterward, I heard the bathroom light click on. It has a distinct sound, because it is the type that you push on or off instead of flipping a switch. Then there was a lady laughing. The next morning, I asked if anyone had gone in the bathroom and found the cat messing around, and everyone said no. They had slept through the night.

GGHG *What is your background with the paranormal? Did it start at an early age or as an adult?*

LH: It started young. I would always hear voices that were coming from nowhere and see things that shouldn't really be there. As I grew older, this became more prominent and happened more often. I have become very interested in the paranormal because of this.

GGHG *What happened on your first formal investigation? Floating heads or a quiet night?*

LH: My first formal investigation was to Greenbottom Cemetery in West Virginia. There were four members of the group there: Rich, Bailey, Megan (Poe), and myself. We separated into two groups. Rich and I started in the back half of the cemetery; Bailey and Poe went down to the front part. At one point, Rich and I started walking across the back side of the cemetery, and as soon as we stopped, we heard a set of heavy footsteps approach us very quickly. They started getting farther away after a while, and we followed after them. We occasionally saw things around a few specific tombstones, so we headed closer to them. Shortly after, we met back up with Bailey and Poe. They were telling us that they had massive K2 (EMF) spikes the whole time. We then decided to switch places. As soon as Rich and I started down the hill to the front side, I started getting this feeling that something was telling me to go to a specific spot. So Rich said, "Lead the way." We finally reached the first spot that I felt pulled to, and my whole body immediately went completely weak, to the point that I almost fell down. I then felt another sensation pulling me over to a tree, and we walked to it. Once we got there, we were both overcome by a strong feeling of dread. It brought tears to both of our eyes. We stayed there for a while, and I found out after we left that apparently Rich was worried about me. He said that he could see me looking at him, but it seemed as if I was looking straight *through* him. Later, we grouped back up. Bailey and Poe informed us that they had used the K2 meter to have a small conversation with the person we had heard up there before. They were led by the spirit to the same tombstone Rich and I had walked to while we were back there. As soon as we left the cemetery, I went from feeling zoned out to having a sudden burst of energy, even though it was midnight.

GGHG *Do you use EVP in your investigations? Do you feel it's an accurate representation of spirit activity or just coincidence?*

LH: Yes, I always carry my EVP recorder with me. I think it is a very amazing way to pick things up. However, you have to have good ears and a solid mind to pick apart sounds and define them as paranormal or fake. If you go about it thinking that every strange little sound is paranormal, then it really isn't a good piece of equipment for you to use. Sometimes, it is better to have more than one person listen to something as well.

GGHG *What are some of your favorite [EVP] interview questions?*

LH: "What is your name?" "Why do you stay here?" "Do you want us to stay?" "Is there something that you need to do?" and, "What happened to you?"

CHAPTER 7

Investigation Boogie, Part 2

YOU'RE THISCLOSE TO BEING ready to roll! This section covers the nitty-gritty on safety for ghost hunts, types of ghosts you may encounter, signs of a haunting, and step-by-step instructions on how to conduct your investigation—plus some other goodies on photos and EVP. (My favorite!) Grab a snack, and let's get crackin'!

SAFETY

This should be the no-brainer section, but let's go over it anyway before you get started. You know the horror movies where a girl walks into an abandoned house, never to be seen again? Yeah. Don't be that girl. Ghost hunting is a hobby that is more fun when shared, so go with a responsible group of friends. And choose them wisely—some people aren't comfortable being faced with the paranormal, so respect their feelings and fill them in afterward. Ask people like this to be a part of the group in another way, such as researching the area, setting up interviews, or updating your website, if you choose to share your experiences online.

Nothing says *newbie* like high heels and a skirt when you're ready to ghost hunt. Jeans, sweaters or sweat-shirts, and sneakers are your best bet when you need to chase down a phantom. You may be crawling into some nasty places like dusty attics or hiking through brush, so be prepared for some wear and tear on your clothes.

Never enter a location without proper permission from the owner—not the guy down the street watering his lawn who said kids go in that house all the time, nor a listing in a book that says the area is thought to be haunted so it's okay for you to look around. No one wants trespassers trampling their roses, so do the right thing and get permission first, either by email, by phone, or in person.

If the location is a public area such as a park, go first in the daytime so you know your way around and how to get back out easily. Follow park rules, and leave when the park closes. The last thing you want is to be trapped

TIP! That growling you hear may not be from a cranky spirit. Make sure you eat something before you leave on your investigation. Always bring snacks and water to help keep you alert and hydrated. Being hungry and thirsty may distract you from the small phenomena that can pop up, so being prepared will keep you ready for action.

behind bars with a ghost or an overly friendly woodland creature.

There's never been a documented case of anyone being physically harmed by a ghost, but that doesn't mean people don't trip over their feet when they are frightened and running away. If you see a floating head, keep yours firmly attached, and don't overreact. Know your surroundings so you don't bump into things in dim lighting, and stay out of cluttered spaces where it's harder to avoid tripping on objects.

If you're outdoors, use your handy compass to get oriented before you head out. It's easy to get caught up in the chase, so make sure you've identified where your base camp is so you can return quickly once you're ready to head back.

Always have an adult with you on an investigation. Not only are adults able to drive you to get pizza afterward, they can be your backup and carry the heavy stuff.

Keep your cell phone with you at all times, but tune out the texting. Things can happen fast during an investigation. Don't miss a minute of it by texting with a friend about what happened at school earlier—share your ghostly experience with her the next day!

TIP! Worried about coming home with some residual ghost stuff stuck to the bottom of your shoe? Don't be. Most ghosts like to hang around the same area, even a whole neighborhood, but they don't want to hitch a ride with visitors.

Use your sixth sense—your common sense. If it moves like a ghost, sounds like a ghost, and smells like a ghost—does that make it a ghost? Not necessarily. Swamp gas, wind, and even gurgling pipes can make an imagination go into overdrive, encouraging people to look over their shoulders and shudder at the thought of a spectral visitor. Research to eliminate the most plausible causes is the first step in ghost hunting. Common sense may be the forgotten sense, but it's invaluable in getting to the bottom of a mystery.

Follow your instincts! You don't need a flaming skull o' doom to tell you when to leave. If you're getting the feeling that you need to mosey out of there, it's probably a good time to wrap things up and return later.

Always be prepared by bringing your ghost hunting kit. Remember that cell phones may not be reliable in all areas, so have a backup plan in case you need to make a quick call.

BOO'S CLUES

Before you head out the door for your newest investigation, what's the best way to get prepared? Take this quiz to sharpen your Yes or Eh-Not-So-Much skills.

YES _or_ EH-NOT-SO-MUCH?

1. I love putting a little extra effort into an investigation by wearing perfume. The stronger the better!

YES   EH-NOT-SO-MUCH

2. T-shirts and jeans are great on an investigation, with a hoodie for when it gets cold at night. Our team had shirts printed with our new logo, so we'll really stand out. I know that if I'm crawling through dusty rooms or standing outside for a while, I'll be more comfortable this way.

YES   EH-NOT-SO-MUCH

3. My new jacket is fabulous! Bright white and slick, it's gorgeous, and I'm going to look perfect in photos! These sparkly earrings will be amazing with it; I'll really stand out.

YES   EH-NOT-SO-MUCH

4. I'm too nervous to eat. What if I see something? What if I puke on my shoes? I won't eat or drink anything so I won't even think about it. Why do I feel woozy anyway? I haven't slept in days. I'm too excited!

YES   EH-NOT-SO-MUCH

5. I love my new shoes. These are going to be great for the ghost hunt. I feel like a cat in them—they're silent and help me climb over rocks without slipping.

YES   EH-NOT-SO-MUCH

6. I am *so* ready for the ghost hunt. I've seen every episode of my favorite ghost hunting team's television show, and I'm ready to get out there and have some fun! What do you mean, I need permission first? They'll never know…!

YES   EH-NOT-SO-MUCH

7. My friends have bailed on me this weekend, so I'll do this on my own. I can't wait to show them what I find…but I wish I didn't have to walk there by myself. I'll leave a note for my parents so they won't worry. Come on, ghosties!

YES   EH-NOT-SO-MUCH

8. I heard some friends talking about a graveyard with ghosts who run around at midnight. I know it's down the road someplace—I'm not sure where, but we'll find it. How many dead people roaming the place can there be?

YES   EH-NOT-SO-MUCH

9. My new ghost detector app for my phone is amazing. It can sense energy all over my house, and I think it'll be great on the investigation. I'm going to save myself a backache and take just that along. Who needs the rest of the stuff anyway?

YES   EH-NOT-SO-MUCH

ANSWERS:

1. EH-NOT-SO-MUCH

Leave the perfume at home. When you're on an investigation, your senses kick into overdrive because you're focused on any paranormal activity that pops up. By wearing perfume, you may be masking some scents that are a way for the ghost to say howdy.

2. YES

Be ready to rumble—with cold, that is. Wearing weather-appropriate clothing not only makes your mom happy that you're not freezing your bottom off out there but that you're ready to deal with any environmental issues like snow and wind. Leave the good clothes at home; ghost hunting can be dirty and sticky, and you'll need to be able to move fast if you're chasing an apparition around the house.

3. EH-NOT-SO-MUCH

You'll stand out, all right. Bright clothing may create reflections in photos, causing investigators to mistake you for a ghost. Be careful of metal jewelry as well; if caught in motion while a photograph is being taken, rings, earrings, and bracelets can all leave traces of glare, creating smears on the picture as the flash goes off. Instead, wear darker, non-reflective clothing on the ghost hunt so you'll be less likely to show up in photos as the Ghost of Investigations Past.

4. EH-NOT-SO-MUCH

Getting ready for a ghost hunt takes a lot of preparation, but don't let taking care of yourself come in second! Make sure you eat something light before going on your adventure, and pack a snack for later. Always have a water bottle ready so you don't get dehydrated.

Your brain can play tricks on you if it's already tired and you're not giving it enough water. Some people may hear or see things that aren't there due to their bodies reacting badly. Make sure you're rested, relaxed, and ready for anything before heading out the door.

5. YES

There's nothing like a great pair of shoes. Even the ugly sneakers your mom got you for gym class can be the perfect pair for ghost hunting if they don't squeak or slide. There's usually a lot of ground to cover during an investigation, so keeping your feet comfortable is important.

6. EH-NOT-SO-MUCH

Always get permission first if going to a privately owned location. If you're going to a public place, follow the posted rules about when it is open for visitors, and stick to them. The police are very aware of the recent popularity of ghost hunting and will not have a problem sending you home with a stern warning (or worse). Pay attention to all signs, so if it says "No Trespassing," it's time to find another location to research and investigate.

7. EH-NOT-SO-MUCH

Always go with a partner or two. Not only will they be there to share the fun, but if something does happen, you'll be able to have someone else around to confirm it too. Sometimes, it happens so quickly that having an extra pair of eyes and ears can help you believe what you may have thought impossible an hour before.

Never go on a ghost hunt without making sure it's okay with your parents first. If they are not going with you, they will need to know whom you're with, what adults will be packing your stuff around, when and where you're going, and when you'll be home, at the very least. A note taped to the fridge won't cut it, Sparky.

8. EH-NOT-SO-MUCH

Finding places to investigate can be as easy as checking your computer or local bookstore. Do your research first before chasing down an urban legend. You'll save time and energy without sitting in a cold, dark graveyard all night listening to crickets. Visit the area in the daytime first so you'll know what the landscape looks like and can avoid things like ditches and areas that may be unsafe. Always have an adult with you, especially at night. Follow your instincts; if any area doesn't feel right, it's not worth the trouble.

9. EH-NOT-SO-MUCH

Apps can be a lot of fun but aren't reliable. It's better to tune your senses toward picking up on the paranormal than to stare at a tiny screen and wait for a blob to float by. Get into the game!

KNOW YOUR GHOSTS

There is no one-size-fits-all type of ghost. One haunting will have a cranky spirit that stomps around at night and knocks on the doors while another will be form an image or repeat a sound weekly at a set time. Learning to tell the difference will help you determine how to deal with your investigation.

Residual Haunting

I once had a case where the homeowner saw a pair of legs in blue woolen pants walk up her driveway daily— only there were no other body parts attached. We determined that because she was living on land in northern Virginia, where the battles of the Civil War had raged, she must have been seeing the residual haunting of a Union soldier coming to her centuries-old house. A residual haunting is a memory trapped in a time loop. Some people are sensitive enough to pick up on the haunting if the time and conditions are right, though a few hauntings are forceful enough to convince even those who don't believe in the paranormal.

Nightly footsteps; habits that were practiced by the ghost before death, such as daily walks or doing the dishes before bed; and even floating heads fall into this category. Reports of a head bobbing along a house corridor were startling until further research found that the house had been remodeled since the time of the person's death, and the ghost was actually traveling down an original staircase or hallway. Observers were simply seeing them with a new wall in the way.

An investigator can't interact with a residual haunting—there is nothing to respond back. You've stumbled into a household memory. Most haunted houses fall within the category of residual hauntings. As an investigator, you will decide whether you're caught in a time warp or have something further to check out—the intelligent haunting.

Intelligent Haunting

Whispered voices caught on tape, cold spots, mist forming into tortured faces, rattling chains in abandoned houses—rare paranormal activity like this exists under the category of intelligent haunting. Ghosts are able to interact with us in these cases; it's their way of reaching out and poking the living to see if anyone pokes back. Intelligent hauntings are what most people think of when they hear of a haunted house.

Film thrives on the idea of these hauntings. After all, how many times can you watch disembodied feet wander up and down the hallway? These cases are best witnessed with a group, as a lot can be going on, and you don't want to miss a thing. And remember—movies make millions because of special effects. Your intelligent haunting may consist of something a bit less spectacular but no less fascinating.

Mediums may be called in to communicate with spirits for intelligent hauntings; their help can sometimes be used to learn more about the entity visiting the house or to convince it to move along, little doggie.

Poltergeist

The word *poltergeist* is German for "noisy ghost." Usually centered around a person between the ages of ten and fourteen years old (heeeey now, why does this sound familiar?), poltergeist activity heats up with drastic intensity in the form of doors slamming on their own, rocks raining on roofs, or other physical evidence that the world has gone crazy.

Research around poltergeist activity may point to either ghosts or a young person unknowingly tapping into the ability to move objects with her mind, usually scaring the pants off themselves in the meantime. The good news is that poltergeist activity is very rare, so any outbursts usually come from you finding the last of the hair conditioner gone instead of anything supernatural.

Random Haunting

Not all hauntings are tied to a particular place. Some may be passing through on their way to their final destination when you get lucky enough to witness them. They may be responsible for a "pop in" haunting of a location that doesn't fit into the residual or intelligent haunting categories as it doesn't return or stick around longer than a few weeks.

Look for this sort of activity if there hasn't been a reported haunting in the area before and there are no other signs of trauma such as an accident scene or deaths.

Shadow People

One of these things ain't like the other hauntings, and girl, it's the Shadow People. Usually caught out of the corner of the eye and popping up just in time to make you drop your popcorn at movie night with the girls, Shadow People put the squeal back in ghost hunting. Often seen as full-bodied dark apparitions with no discernable features—such as, oh, I don't know, how about a face?—these beings fade out of view as quickly as they appear. Ghost researchers are only now beginning to classify them as their own sub-category of paranormal activity.

Haunted Possessions

Spirits may attach themselves to objects, as well as locations and people. The doll you wanted on eBay? Double-check its history; you may get more than you bargained for if the first owner isn't ready to give it up yet.

When doing your investigative research, ask the home-owners if they've recently brought home a new item. Chairs, beds, and cars have long memories, even if their past owners have moved on. Jewelry seems to have special ties to a haunting; those diamonds didn't just fall out of the sky, Sparky.

SiGNS OF A HAUNTiNG

In another case I helped investigate, homeowners often heard an elderly lady doing the dishes late at night and then thumping up the stairs, using her cane to help her old bones manage the climb. In the morning, they were disappointed to see that any dishes left in the sink from the night before remained in the sink; they were looking forward to one less chore. Was the haunting really a ghost or just wishful thinking?

Some of the signs that an area may have paranormal activity include:

Sounds

Footsteps: More common in residual hauntings, footsteps may replay a path taken by a long-dead resident, pacing the floors at night when it's quiet or even running up and down the stairs. These spectral wanderings should be recorded when and where they happen to see if there's a pattern.

Doors opening or shutting: There's nothing like the soft click of a doorknob when you know you're alone in the house to get the blood pumping! Hearing a door move is more common than seeing it open or shut. You may have wandered into a memory of a ghost coming home after a long day at work.

Knocking: Rapping or pounding on the walls will definitely get your attention. If this occurs, try to pinpoint where the sounds are coming from to investigate.

Music: Phantom music has been featured in many ghost experiences through instruments such as a piano or violin or through the radio—even if these items aren't in the house. Keep an ear out for what song is playing. If you can identify the tune, it may help you to place the time period the ghost is trapped in.

Crying: Sometimes, a ghost just needs a hug.

Voices or whispers: Late at night, when the house is quiet, you may be able to hear someone telling you not to forget your science proooojeeecccttt—

General noises: Note sounds that you can't identify, such as grunting or clicks. Be sure to eliminate all other possible reasons for those noises first before deciding they are paranormal. Rodents in the walls, air in the pipes, or wind against the windows are common causes of strange noises, especially in older houses.

Screaming: Nothing like a bloodcurdling scream to make you whip out your logbook! Well, after you've stopped running, that is. A burst of energy like this isn't common, so try to discover where the scream originated from and try to learn why it happened then and there.

Smells

Cigars, pipes, or cigarettes: The smell of tobacco can be so strong that it stains the air. If you are in an area that does not allow smoking or can determine that there is no one close who is smoking, write down when and where you first smelled the smoke. While visiting the Whaley House in San Diego, California, I noticed the scent of a cigar in the museum. I learned a short time later that the ghost of the former owner was often sensed by the heavy smell of cigars he'd smoked while alive.

Food: Just what did your mother put in that casserole? Since the kitchen is the heart of the home, a lot of memories are associated with food and the way it's prepared. I know I've been haunted by the thought of chocolate chip cookies…

Perfume: Known as perfume ghosts, some spirits have been identified by the presence of a scent they wore during life, such as the ghost at the Octagon House in

Washington, D.C., who smells of lilacs as she passes by the living.

Gunpowder: There have been reports of the smell of gunpowder from the battlefields of Gettysburg, Pennsylvania, on days when there have been no reenactments.

The Winchester Mystery House in California smells of chicken soup on occasion. I wonder if we could convince the ghost to make biscuits.

Visions

To see something appear from nowhere or watch something scoot across the floor on its own can give you a pretty good heads-up that something's afoot.

Movement seen out of the corner of the eye: Small, fleeting glimpses of shadows are frequently noted in paranormal cases. Too quick to be seen clearly, they disappear before the living can get a good look. Be sure to rule out headlights from passing cars, shadows created by clouds, and toddlers who are much too fast for their own good.

Apparitions: Seeing a full-body apparition is incredibly rare, so if it happens, try to remember what it was wearing so you can identify the time period later. Also note it was making any motions or facial expressions and if there were any sounds happening at the same time. Some apparitions are merely wisps of smoke, while others so closely resemble the living that they've been mistaken for someone with a pulse.

Electrical appliances switched off and on: This includes televisions, lights, ovens, and game systems. On lamps, check for touch-light bulbs—these lamps may be tricky and turn themselves on and off due to faulty wiring. Have an adult check for frayed wires before you think it's a ghost.

Items are moved: You know you left your homework by the door, so why isn't it there when you're running out the door for the bus? In some cases, items go missing, only to pop up someplace else at a later date. Sometimes, a ghost may bring things to your house that you've never seen before, such as coins or jewelry.

Heads floating: Just wanted to see if you were paying attention.

Once More...with Feeling

Feelings of being watched: Downright creepy. 'Nuff said.

Nightmares: Ghosts may find it easier to communicate through the dream state, as it takes less energy than writing their names on the wall—though it's much less dramatic. If you are having multiple nightmares, take control and note what symbols or feelings may be present that you can identify later. Happiness? It may be a loved one saying a final good-bye. Dread? What are you worried about? A ghost may be there to help you work through it and find some answers.

Unexplained cold spots: Is there an area of the house that is noticeably colder than the rest of the room? Check for open vents or drafts first. See if you can discover the area's shape; some are tall and thin, while others have wobbly shapes and ill-defined borders. If you've walked into a cold spot, make sure the air conditioning is turned off and poke a hand into it one more time. If the spot is still present, pull out your mercury thermometer and try to get a reading. Don't forget to log it in your book!

Pets

Animals can be excellent partners in investigating the paranormal. By noting their reactions to rooms or areas thought to be haunted, you may be able to tell if there is activity. Then you can pull out your camera and start clicking away!

QUIZ
GHOST CRITERIA

You're walking down the hall, munching on an apple, when something catches the corner of your eye. Reflection? Rebel hamster out of his cage? Naked baby sister? Or the spiritual residue of someone who should have been buried long ago? Ghosts fall into three categories.

☻ A vision of someone still alive

☻ An apparition of someone near death who wants to give loved ones a final wave good-bye

☻ A person who's been dead for a while but still likes to pop in and say howdy

So if you bump into something in the hallway, how can you tell if you should investigate further or just go back to bed? The Society for Psychical Research has been studying the paranormal since 1882 and came up with some of these criteria to help sort out paranormal phenomena from a bad burrito.

CHECKLiST for a GHOST:

○ Does it float through solid objects like doors or walls?

○ Is it able to disappear while you're watching it?

○ Does it make your pet go nuts, even if it's not visible?

○ Can it let itself be seen and heard to some people and not to others?

○ Does it go about its business as if you're not there or try to communicate with you in some way such as automatic writing or whispers?

○ Does it creep you out, making its presence known by watching you, often from behind?

○ Does it come with its own spectral air conditioner, making the room temperature drop?

○ Is it sometimes solid to the touch (ew)?

○ Do you see it reflected in mirrors?

Does it leave no trace, such as footprints?

Are you able to walk through it or pass a hand through its body without trouble (double ew)?

Is it camera shy, or does it show up on film or video?

TOP FOUR FAMOUS GHOSTS

hey had it all: power, glamour—they even drank fruity drinks with little umbrellas in them while lounging at the pool—so why are they back and what do they want?

1 ABRAHAM LINCOLN: Sure, he wore a hat named after part of a kitchen appliance, but the sixteenth president of the United States had his fingers in the paranormal pie. On the night of his presidential election, Lincoln was reported to have had a double vision of himself in a mirror—one healthy and strong but the other, pale as death, in the reflection. See, I told you mirrors were ominous.

His wife, Mary Todd Lincoln, became a supporter of the Spiritualist movement, inviting mediums to hold séances at the White House, but Lincoln didn't need outside help. One night, he awoke from a dream where he'd seen a coffin surrounded by weeping crowds in the East Room of the White House. When he asked a nearby guard who lay dead in the room, the guard responded that it was the president who had been assassinated. Days later, Lincoln was murdered at Ford's Theater. Coincidence? I think not.

The ghost of Lincoln is now said to haunt the White House. During their administrations, Presidents Theodore Roosevelt, Herbert Hoover and Harry Truman heard strange knocking upon their bedroom doors attributed to their presidential predecessor, and old Abe has been known to pop in on foreign dignitaries who were guests in the White House.

2 ELVIS PRESLEY: You didn't think the King of Rock and Roll would fade quietly into the night, did you? Any man that can shake his bad thing in a white sequined jumpsuit does nothing halfway, including haunting the old RCA Records building in Nashville, Tennessee, where he recorded his hit, "Heartbreak Hotel." The television crews that work there now say that every time someone mentions Presley's name, paranormal activity kicks up some dust, along with lights exploding, mysterious noises, and ladders tipping over.

Elvis has also been spotted at his home in Memphis, Tennessee, at Graceland, and rockin' the halls at the Las Vegas Hilton. That man can't just leave the building quietly, can he?

3 MARILYN MONROE: The 1950s movie bombshell launched a million Halloween costumes in the past fifty years with her sassy blond hair and curvy figure, but after her death from an accidental overdose in 1962, Monroe couldn't stay away from adoring fans. She has been seen visiting the home where she died in Hollywood, California, and will occasionally appear in the full-length mirror that formerly hung in her room at the Hollywood Roosevelt Hotel. The mirror is currently in the lobby of the hotel; dare to try to see her yourself?

4 MICHAEL JACKSON: What is it with singers? The King of Pop came to an untimely death in 2009 but refuses to leave his vast Neverland estate no matter how many times Bubbles the chimp tells him to go to the light. The Cable News Network (CNN) captured what appeared to be a shadow wandering the halls of Neverland while filming a report for talk show host Larry King. A reporter from the United Kingdom claimed to have seen Jackson's face reflected in the hood of a car while he was on assignment at the ranch.

LET THE INVESTIGATION BEGIN!

Now comes the fun part. Your research is done, you've talked to the homeowners and witnesses—it's time to poke the unknown and see if it giggles.

Before you begin, go over the rules:

1. No one goes in or out of an area alone. Aside from safety reasons, you'll want someone there to nod vigorously when you tell everyone about the ghost that just waved to you in the next room.

2. Respect personal property. If you're in a private home, leave everything as you found it. If you need a piece of equipment from a team member's kit, ask first before digging in.

3. Always be dressed to investigate. No perfume, no gum, no sassy but impractical shoes, and always tie back long hair before taking any photos.

4. In a private home, always act professionally. Clients will be more likely to invite you back if you show that you're prepared to take their stories seriously.

5. In a public area, have a set time to check in and a central meeting location if you split up to cover a large location. Agree on the time to leave before starting the investigation so every investigator will be ready to pack up on time. Have cell phone numbers already on speed dial in case of emergency and phones set to vibrate in your pocket.

Let's get started!

Indoor Investigations

The team leader will divide members into teams of two or three. Everyone gets a buddy for backup. Each member should have their own ghost hunting kit with them, or at least a camera, notepad, pencil, and watch. Make sure the team is up to date on all recent ghostly activity, and break into groups.

PRIVATE RESIDENCES

When you arrive, greet the homeowners, and thank them for having your team come. Use graph paper to map the areas you'll be investigating, so you'll know the layout of the rooms. If there are particular pieces of furniture that seem to get a bit jumpy on their own, make note of that on the map so you can check later to see if they've moved. If you wish, wrap a piece of string around the base of the item to help determine if it's gone wandering.

f you're investigating a very large outdoor area, stick together as a group with your adult. Chasing down lost team members can be a safety issue and is not recommended.

Ask the homeowners to close all windows and turn off the heater or air conditioner, if possible. If there are known drafts, ask them to point those out to the team so no one thinks they're feeling a breeze from the beyond. Note the appliances that have humming motors, such as refrigerators and furnaces. They can throw off your EVP recordings if you're standing too close.

If there are interviews to conduct, have your interviewer do them in a separate room while the others are busy mapping and getting their equipment ready.

TICK...TICK...TICK

Ah, the glamour. Most of ghost hunting is spent sitting for long periods of time waiting for something exciting to happen. Keep a sharp eye out, and use your logbook to record any phenomena. I know it's tempting to chat with your partner, but it's easy to get distracted and miss something subtle, such as knocking or a cold spot, so wait until the ride home to compare notes on a history test.

Visit an area in the daylight before the investigation starts so you can map out where the exits are, if there are rooms the homeowner does not want you to explore, and if there are other geographical details near the area, such as bodies of water, caverns, or your run-of-the-mill ancient American Indian burial ground.

After twenty to thirty minutes, change rooms or stations with your other team members; a fresh pair of eyes can make a difference. If you don't feel there is activity in one area, feel free to switch rooms after the time is up, if the Lead Investigator agrees.

WHAT WAS THAT?

Now isn't the time for running in small circles—save that for later! If you do see or hear something, try to pinpoint where the action is. Keep your logbook ready to record when, where, and for how long the phenomena lasted.

Sounds: Was it loud or soft? Near to you or perhaps in another room or hallway? On another floor? Did anyone else hear the sound, and where do they think it came from?

Footsteps: Were they sounds like boots stomping around? Bare feet?

Knocking or rapping: Did the knocking stay in one place or did it travel around the room? Can you duplicate where it came from and how loud it sounded? Check for natural causes such as furniture being moved by the family, trees bumping against the house, or clumsy fellow investigators.

Speaking or whispers: Very dramatic to hear but always fun. I once had a ghost grunt in my ear while I chased him around a room. I checked with my team members to see if they had possibly been giving me a sign to move it on over and get out of the way, but they both shook their heads. *Eep!*

If you hear a sweet nothing from the beyond, check if others heard it as well, and mark it down in your logbook with the room and time it happened. Then whip out that voice recorder and see if they get chatty!

Physical changes: Physical changes may include moving objects, such as a chair rocking by itself, doors slamming, windows rattling, or things floating. If possible, video record what happens to analyze later.

TIP: Now is a good time to try recording EVPs!

Emotional changes: Some investigators have experienced feelings of anger, overwhelming joy, or melancholy during a ghost hunt. If this happens, leave the room for a bit, and get some fresh air. It's thought that some ghosts can affect moods, so if you're very sensitive to others' feelings, take a break and return when you're ready.

Atmospheric changes: Brrr, what the heck? Noticeably different temperature-wise than the rest of the room, cold or hot spots have been identified as signs of a haunting. If you can determine that there's no other way for the room to have changed—such as air conditioning or a draft—you may have walked into a ghost.

Use your hands to feel the shape of the spot. Some may be quite large; record the estimated size in your logbook, plus if it was colder or hotter than the rest of the room. If you have a thermometer with you, go ahead and stick it in there to see what the temperature difference is from the rest of the room—but I think you'll be able to tell if it's frosty or not.

Sight: Is seeing believing? Your mind will probably doubt what your eyes see, but train that brain to kick in, and use your investigative skills.

If you're lucky enough to come face to face with a ghost, stay still and record the following:

TIP! If you've brought pieces of equipment such as EMF detectors, test them on the area when you arrive so you'll know where the outlets are rather than just thinking the blender is just super happy to see them when the EMF detector spikes.

What was the shape of the ghost? Is it formed like a human? A blob of mist? A body part like a hand or head?

What direction was it going? Toward you or away from you? Did it go into another room, float upward, head to the kitchen for a snack? What? Ghosts get the munchies too…

TIP! Don't forget to take a team-wide break for snacks! A weary ghost hunter is likely to miss the little things so a ten-minute break each hour is a great way to stretch your legs and check in with your other teammates. Get some fresh air, refill your water bottle and bust out the granola bars!

Did it seem to know you were there? Residual hauntings follow their own loops, and won't notice if they pass right through you. Intelligent hauntings may interact with a "S'up" nod, whisper in your ear, or throw you a wink. They can be quite silly.

Did it change shape or color or become more solid as you watched? Be sure to have your camera and voice recorder ready, as these sightings aren't common. When it fades away, write down as much as you can in your logbook, and check your digital camera to see if you were able to capture your ghost. Play back your voice recordings in case they left you a little message before leaving.

Smells: Mmm, nothing could be finer than the scent of—hey, wait a minute, what does a ghost smell like anyway? While ghosts don't have a particular odor, some may be associated with smells like cooking food, cleaning products, tobacco products like cigars and pipes, flowers, and even rotting eggs. If you notice something wafting from the rafters, write down where it came from or if it was suddenly all over the room, how long it lasted, and if the scent has been linked to a ghost reported in the area already. Some ghosts are identified when they arrive by the scent they carry. Hopefully, it's roses instead of stinky feet. Just sayin'.

t's easy to get a little cramped while waiting for a ghost. If you do start moving around or knock things over, be sure to tell your teammates, so they don't think you're part of the floor show.

Outdoor Investigations

If you're going out to a public area, such as a cemetery or park, check the weather before you start. Wind, moisture, and woodland creatures can all affect your investigation. Be sure to visit the area in the daytime if you're planning an evening ghost hunt, so you're aware of landmarks that can help you stay on the paths and avoid tripping over broken headstones or exposed tree roots.

Go over the tips listed above, and adapt them to your hunt. You may hear whispers in the wind instead of directly in your ear, or that white glow you've been chasing could turn out to be a rabbit (it happens). It's easy to get distracted outdoors, so pay attention to the little things!

Wrapping It Up

With luck, you will have filled your logbook with goodies and photos to pore over after you get home. Pack away your equipment, and double-check that you left nothing behind. Thank the homeowners, and head home.

QUESTION FROM A FUTURE GHOST HUNTER

CAN GHOSTS TOUCH YOU?
Wynter G., age 12

I've had my nose tickled and hair pulled, and a hand ran down my back the night after my first human ghost appeared, so yes, they can touch you. There's never been a documented case of a ghost actually hurting a living person, however, so don't worry that they're doing more than giving you the stink eye if they're cranky.

FREEZE FRAME: GETTING YOUR GHOST TO SAY "CHEESE."

Whip out those cameras, ladies!

Before you start:

- 💀 **Tie back your hair** so no strands get in the way of the camera lens.

- 💀 **Check the weather conditions** before you head out. While a foggy night is excellent for a spooky atmosphere, the fog can create shapes in your photos that may be mistaken for ghosts. Clear or overcast nights are best.

- 💀 **Don't wear clothing that is reflective or bright.** Super white coats against a dark night can make reflections bounce back to the camera.

- 💀 **Double-check that your digital camera is charged** and has enough memory before you start clicking. Ghosts have an annoying habit of draining batteries. Keep a charger or extra batteries in the car so you can get back to the fun.

- 💀 **Take more than one type of camera.** If you're using a digital, bring along a 35mm or disposable camera as well to use as backup.

Ready? Awesome—let's get snappin', but first some tips:

☠ **Watch those fingers,** because it's easy for a thumb or pinkie to sneak into a photo. Keep your digits curled around the camera and away from the lens.

☠ **If you're indoors,** check for anything that may cause a reflection, and cover it up or note its position in your logbook. Then when you check your pictures later, you can tell if it's an anomaly or a collection of mirrored disco balls. Some things to check for:

○ Mirrors   ○ Windows

○ Kitchen utensils or pans   ○ Television sets

○ Shiny knickknacks   ○ Polished wooden furniture

☠ **If you have a camera with a strap,** put your hand through the loop to keep it from straying into the picture. If it wanders in front of the lens, the light from the flash may bounce back into the camera, and the strap may be mistaken for a long ghostly blob called a vortex.

☠ **If you think there's something giving you the stink eye,** stand still and take a few photos of that area, one right after the other. Taking more than one photo at a time can prove that it was a reflection if you get a glare in the same spot. You may also catch a ghost moonwalking…

If you're taking EVPs, have a team member take photos of the room at the same time to see who's chatting you up.

A Real Ghost or a Giant Bug?

Cameras have developed (snicker) in the digital age, so while you're less likely to have double exposures like in previous decades, here are two photographic tricks that can fool your eyes into seeing something that's not there.

Dust: Once thought by those in the biz to be physical proof of ghosts, most orbs in photographs are now known to be dust particles, mold spores, moisture, reflections, or the glare of the flash off of a bug you've just blinded as you took the photo. Dust is everywhere. Even the most airtight rooms can't get rid of those tiny particles, so is it any wonder that they get kicked up in dusty old houses or outside? To help reduce the amount of fluff kicked up before you take your photos, stick to a spot and stay there for a few minutes to let the dust settle.

Sequins: They can be awesome—just not on a ghost hunt. If someone is wearing something sparkly, such as reflective beads or jewelry, ask them to remove them before the cameras come out to reduce the chance of the flash creating false images. Remember—no bling at the fling.

PHANTOM OR FAKE?

When weird things start to happen, it's important to stop, take a deep breath, and take a close look at what's really going on. Most paranormal activity can be easily explained by natural causes such as animals or weather, so don't lose your head, even if you see a floating apparition coming at ya. Okay, you have my permission to run if *that* happens.

Sometimes, it's not so easy to tell if what you're seeing is real or if your mind is playing tricks on you. That's when your investigative skills kick in, and it's time to whip out your notebook.

Need a little reminder? Think of your friendly neighborhood chicken:

HENS

HANDS. Can you feel a cold or hot spot? What is the temperature in the room? Tuning in to your sense of touch can be a big help in determining the overall vibe of a room, since when you're focused on ghosts, you may become more in tune with your environment.

EYES. What can you tell about the phenomenon? Did you see something scoot across the room? If it's a ghost, what is it wearing? Many times, investigations are done in dimly lit rooms and your eyes can trick you into thinking you've seen something that wasn't actually there. Always stick with a buddy who may be able to confirm what you've seen.

NOSE. Is there a smell that suddenly appeared? Can it be traced back to a person who is currently standing near you, or is it dinnertime in the neighborhood? Sometimes, supper smells can waft in through an open window or vent and make you think you've stepped into a paranormal event…and make you hungry too!

SOUNDS. Can you pinpoint the source of the sound? Rodents can wiggle up walls and beneath floorboards, so be sure to ask if the family has had problems with pests before. If you think you hear something, start recording an EVP session, and see if you can pick up more on what they're chatting about. You may find that it's simply someone downstairs looking for fruity cereal at midnight.

ELECTRONIC VOICE PHENOMENA

To give yourself a serious case of the willies, try your hand at capturing electronic voice phenomena (EVP). You know how dogs can hear whistles outside of human hearing? EVPs work along similar paths. Those whispers you "thought" you heard coming from your closet may be something after all. One theory is that living humans are not in tune with ghosts' "frequency," so we can't pick up on when they're trying to get our attention. EVP recordings are one way paranormal investigators try to communicate with ghosts.

EVP

Using a voice recorder, you may be able to pick up on that ghost doing interpretive dance in the corner. Ask questions clearly, pausing between them so you can hear your answer.

HOW TO DO IT:

1. Using a handheld device such as a mini-voice recorder, begin your investigation by speaking clearly into the microphone. State your name, date, location, and who is with you. When you move to another room, don't forget to update your location into the recorder so you don't get places mixed up!

2. Ask questions as you walk around the area. "What is your name? Your age? What was happening at the time of your death (so you can find out when they died)?" Get creative; you never know what they'll come back with.

3. Some noises are human-made and can't be helped while recording: a car outside, someone coughing, tripping over a table in the dark. Be sure to record anything like that in your notes and on the voice recording so you won't think it's a ghost later.

4. When you've finished asking your questions, stop the recording, and play it back when you have a quiet moment. Be sure to take notes and share the recording with the other investigators for their interpretation.

Some investigators stop to listen before they move on to the next room or location, just in case a ghost is trying give them a high-five. You'd hate to get all the way home and realize you left a ghost hangin'!

Noises to listen for:

* Obvious voices that are not from your team
* Breathing
* Scratching
* Static
* Animals
* Unidentifiable noises

It's easy to mistake a team member's whisper about needing a snack for a phantom's noise, so remember to have only one person speaking at a time.

TIP! Try running water in the background or tuning a radio to play only "white noise," or static. Some researchers theorize that ghosts may have a better chance at saying howdy if they use background noise.

GHOST BOX

arty Seibel of the Shenandoah Valley Paranormal Society (SVPS) explains how his group uses the latest tool in ghost hunting, the ghost box, in addition to taking EVPs during investigations:

MS: A ghost box is a tool used by some paranormal investigators to communicate or speak with the other side. Basically, a ghost box is a modified, portable AM/FM radio that continuously scans the bands. It is believed to create white noise and audio remnants from broadcast stations that entities are able to use to form words and complete sentences to communicate with the living.

SVPS experiments using the ghost box in investigations before and after regular EVP sessions. Initially skeptical of the ghost box, we have had more and more interesting results within the past six months.

We were skeptical because first and foremost this is radio, and second, a lot of times, people can hear what they want to hear. However, we have had some very clear, immediate responses, some intelligent, that have made us turn our heads and think, "Maybe there is something more to this."

GGHG: *What has been the most memorable response you've received from the ghost box?*

MS: My most memorable quotes from the ghost box have been it saying my name without asking just after I had conducted a regular EVP session in Fort Mifflin (Philadelphia) in which I had introduced myself. It was very clear.

We have had some immediate responses on our ghost tours called Ghosts of Staunton in Staunton, Virginia, during the anniversary of an 1890 train wreck, which killed seventeen-year-old Miss Myrtle Knox. We now conduct ghost box sessions on each and every tour, and we have our customers, as well as our guides, ask questions. We have had a few very clear, intelligent, female responses come across immediately after questions were asked.

FAST FIVE TIPS FROM GHOST HUNTER LAMISHIA ALLEN OF WEE GHOSTIES

1 *Hunt in teams of at least two.* Never investigate alone; safety first.

2 *Be vigilant.* It is in the times that seem boring that things start to happen, so pay attention.

3 *Always document information.* Make sure you note the time of hearing or observing phenomena.

4 *Look up, look down, look all around.* Change up your point of view. It would be awful to miss an disembodied spirit because it appeared over your head.

5 *Try, try again.* Just because you get nothing on your first investigation doesn't mean there isn't anything to be heard or seen at a location. Come back at a different time, day, or season, and try again.

QUIZ

WHAT KIND OF GHOST IS IT?

After an hour or two of sitting in a dark room waiting for something to happen, it's easy to let your guard down. But when you take your mind off your butt cramp and stretch your legs, that's when things get hopping. Can you figure out what kind of ghost is getting into the cookie jar when you least expect it?

Match the name of the ghost with its description below.

A. Full-bodied apparitions

B. Intelligent hauntings

C. Mist or fog hauntings

D. Pets

E. Phantom vehicles

F. Poltergeists

G. Residual hauntings

H. Shadow people

1. The walls, they are a shakin', the dog is hiding under the bed, and there is one very cranky thirteen-year-old unable to download her favorite song. One of the more frightening paranormal phenomena, these ghosts throw a temper tantrum that makes the neighbors edge a little closer to moving when it gets stirred up. It's believed that some of the activity may stem from the subconscious minds of teenagers, though don't use that excuse with your mom if your room gets trashed.

2. Nothing says "I like you" the way that a ghost popping up and following you into the bathroom at 4 a.m. does. While these ghosts can be a bit on the friendly side, don't confuse them with your cat. Usually large, dark, and mysterious, this ghost type can be classified as one of those things that make you go, "Hmmm?" Or scream and throw things at the wall. Whatever.

3. The most rarely seen ghost type, they make the best ghost stories. With what other ghost can you stare into the gaping eyeholes of a skull with long flowing hair? Okay, ick. These ghosts may be seen in the clothes they died or were buried in, so try to remember what they were wearing to help place a date for your ghostie.

.... **4.** Hearing lullabies while a cradle is rocked by an unseen hand every night? These ghosts make their presence known without all the showing off, like some of the other spirits. One of the more commonly reported types of phenomena, they're trapped in a loop like a giant hamster wheel. A *ghostly* hamster wheel. Yes, I went there.

.... **5.** Not much is nicer than a soft fuzzy creature showing its love by rubbing up against you—unless that creature died years ago and you're kind of squicked out by the whole idea of a phantom feline. These ghosts are one of the more welcome spirits to return and say howdy.

.... **6.** How the heck did fog get into the house? While the weather outside might be frightful on some investigations, these ghosts manifest, or appear, by forming a mist or fog that has nothing to do with the temperature.

.... **7.** The rock stars of paranormal phenomena, these bad boys can be chatty, annoying, and fascinating at the same time. Able to interact with the living, these ghosts keep the investigator coming back to see what they'll do next.

.... **8.** Not a person or a place but a thing. These ghosts show up but have no floating heads to pack around. If a spectral car pulls up and offers a ride, tell it to hit the road, Jack.

La Llorona

What could be scarier than a woman wandering near riverbanks looking for children to kidnap and drown? Not much, my friend. The legend of La Llorona, or "the Weeping Woman," is very much alive in Mexico and the American Southwest. Be on the lookout for this one if you're out after dark…

Many years ago, Maria was born in a small rural village in Mexico. Drop-dead gorgeous, she grew up spoiled and proud and rejected the local men in an effort to save herself for someone who would appreciate her unique brand of awesomeness. Luckily for her, the son of a wealthy rancher rode into town and was smitten by Maria, and they quickly married. Years passed, and her husband grew bored of her selfishness. He returned to his former life of drinking and gambling while leaving her at home with their two children. Maria grew to resent the boys, for when her husband returned, it was only to see his sons, and not to give her the attention she felt she deserved. Bitterness consumed her, her beauty faded, and the realization that the man she loved might leave her forever began to drive her nutty.

One day, as she walked with the boys by the river, she spied her husband driving their carriage nearby. Coming closer, she saw a woman seated next to him. Maria knew this woman, well dressed and elegant as she was, had come from a rich family, one that had a dowry to offer to pay off her husband's gambling debts if he could get rid of his inconvenient wife.

Stopping the carriage, he spoke to the boys while ignoring Maria, then rode on. Maria, in a fit of rage at the inevitability of being left for another woman, went completely bonkers. She threw her children into the river to drown, making her husband pay for his betrayal. As the boys were swept farther into the water and away from her reach, she realized what she had done and ran down the riverbank screaming, her long black hair coming loose from its bun and streaming behind her, tangling in the wind.

"Mis niños!" she cried. But there was no answer.

She returned home, desperate for help to rescue the two young boys, but when she told her husband what had happened, she saw that his heart had left her completely, and he threw her out into the street. Weeks passed, and as she scoured the river for signs of her children, she grew thin as madness clawed at her mind, as well as starving her body.

"Mis niños!" she'd cry—and was met with only silence.

One morning the townspeople found her lying on the ground next to the river. She had died from a broken heart, though the lack of food probably didn't help much. She was wrapped in a long, white gown and buried in a local churchyard. Soon afterward, her ghost was seen again on the riverbank, frantically searching for the boys. The townspeople grew afraid of her, as she'd approach children at night, thinking they were her own. Floating toward them, her eyes wild, her hands reached out to grab them, only to throw them into the river to drown. Other times, people would spy her wading in the river, her white gown flowing around her as she scraped the water with her arms in search of her sons and screamed for them to return to her.

La Llorona has been seen multiple times around the Santa Fe River area, though she has been reported as far north as the banks of the Yellowstone River in Montana. Could it be the cry of foxes that sound like the weeping woman, or is it really poor Maria, still in search of her sons? Her story has been repeated as a cautionary tale to children who wander late at night: would you take a chance at meeting the Weeping Woman?

QUESTION FROM A FUTURE GHOST HUNTER

IS THERE ANYTHING WE CAN DO TO HELP GHOSTS NOT BE MAD OR WANT TO HAUNT US?
Hana K., age 11

Not all ghosts are mad; in fact, I don't think most ghosts know even we're crowding their space. A lot of hauntings are residual, meaning sort of a memory loop, and we've stepped into that memory. There is no real "ghost" in such instances—just a slight hiccup in time. In intelligent hauntings, you may be able to interact with ghosts or sense their antics, such as closing doors or whispering to you, but they may not even be aware that you're there.

Ghosts' personalities are much like they were during their lifetimes. If they were grumpy before they died, it's a good bet that they're not cuddly now. Some ghosts may be tied to an area due to how they died; if it was violent or dramatic, they may not know they're dead. You can help by telling them in a firm voice that it's time to mosey along—though this may take more than one attempt—ghosts are notoriously stubborn.

BREAKIN' IT DOWN

After the fun of the investigation, it's time to look at your notes, photographs, and voice recordings to see if you've found something giving you a high-five from the other side.

Logbook

Go over the data to see if you can find a pattern forming, such as seeing a mist every hour or an object move in a specific path. Are there certain times when there's more activity than others?

Photographs

Upload your photos to your computer to get a better look at what you snapped during the ghost hunt. It can be easy to mistake a friend's backpack for something floating in the distance, so give yourself plenty of time to zoom in on a picture and really analyze what something is before automatically thinking it's a ghost. Write down the time, date, and place where the photograph was taken in your logbook so you can keep your notes together. If you have photo-enhancing software, play around a bit with the brightness levels to see if there is something lurking in the background. Note if there is anything really out of the ordinary like mist, floating fingers, or giant whirlpools of ectoplasm.

Audio and Video

EVP: Get comfy—this could take a while. EVPs can take the form of whispers, grunts, screaming, low talking, growling—you get the picture. Grab your favorite pair of earphones and settle down as you decipher the little nibbles of communication that may come through your recordings. If you hear something that is obviously not one of your teammates or outside interference, such as a car or plane, write it down in your notes, along with the timestamp. After finishing the audio loop, go back and listen again. Check to see if it's something you can explain, like kitchen appliances, dogs barking outside, or neighbors chatting near an open window.

Videos: If you've taken a video camera with you on your investigation, break out the popcorn and settle in. Look for signs of movement in objects such as chandeliers and chairs, as well as small trinkets that pop up when no one is in the room. Keep an eye out for lights or mist that may zip around when your back is turned; ghosts can be infamously sneaky.

If you do find something, check your logbook to see if you've made a note about an occurrence happening at the same time. The lights you see bouncing off the ceiling could be car lights reflecting off a mirror in another room, or a teammate walking heavily upstairs could be making the chandelier swing. The simplest, most common-sense solution is usually right!

After your post-investigation party is complete, share your results with your teammates and compare what you've found. If you heard weird mumblings on your EVP recordings, double-check that the investigator in the next room wasn't humming along to her iPod and picked up by accident. A new pair of eyes can also detect what yours missed, so trade photos and video so everyone can confirm what you've seen. If your evidence could possibly have a reasonable and natural (not supernatural) explanation, try to recreate the occurrence the next time you visit the location.

SHARING THE LOVE

After all the logbooks, photographs, and audio-visual evidence have been shared, make copies to be kept by the team leader or record keeper. If you are investigating a private house, write up what you've found to give to the homeowner. If you found nothing that couldn't be explained, let them know what you did find that may give them some answers. If you were lucky enough to capture something in photographs, videos, or EVP recordings, share that with them, if they'd like to see it. Some home-owners aren't comfortable with the thought of sharing the house with someone who doesn't pay rent or do chores, so if they choose not to hear about the ghost in their closet, just smile and thank them for the opportunity to investigate.

Conclusion

I HATE TO SAY good-bye, so let's wrap up *The Girls' Ghost Hunting Guide* with some bad jokes:

WHAT DO YOU GET iF YOU CROSS A COCKER SPANiEL, A POODLE, AND A GHOST?

A cocker-poodle-boo!

WHAT KiND OF MAKEUP DO GHOSTS WEAR?

Mas-scare-a!

WHAT KiND OF ROADS DO GHOSTS HAUNT?

Dead ends!

Had enough yet?

Okay, one more—

WHERE DOES A GHOST GO
ON SATURDAY NiGHT?

Anywhere where he can boo-gie!

Now I'm done.

➡ LOGBOOK

Things may move quickly during an investigation, so try to remember to write things down as soon as possible after they happen.

CASE ADDRESS: ....
....
....

DATE: .... TIME: ....

ROOM OR LOCATION: ....

HOW LONG DID IT LAST? ....

WHO WAS WITH YOU? ....
....

WAS IT COLD OR HOT AT THE TIME? ....

DID YOU SMELL ANYTHING? ....
....

DID YOU FEEL ANYTHING? ....
....

DID YOU HEAR ANYTHING? ....

....

WHAT EQUIPMENT DID YOU USE? ....

....

PHOTOS TAKEN IN WHAT ROOM/AREA? ....

> WHAT TIME? ....

> WHAT WERE THE WEATHER CONDITIONS, IF OUTSIDE? ....

....

EVPS RECORDED: ....

> WHAT TIME? ....

> WHAT ROOM/AREA? ....

SO WHAT HAPPENED? ....

....

....

....

....

....

....

....

LOGBOOK

Things may move quickly during an investigation, so try to remember to write things down as soon as possible after they happen.

CASE ADDRESS: ....
....
....

DATE: .... TIME: ....

ROOM OR LOCATION: ....

HOW LONG DID IT LAST? ....

WHO WAS WITH YOU? ....
....

WAS IT COLD OR HOT AT THE TIME? ....

DID YOU SMELL ANYTHING? ....
....

DID YOU FEEL ANYTHING? ....
....

DID YOU HEAR ANYTHING? ....

....

WHAT EQUIPMENT DID YOU USE? ....

....

PHOTOS TAKEN IN WHAT ROOM/AREA? ....

> WHAT TIME? ....

> WHAT WERE THE WEATHER CONDITIONS, IF OUTSIDE? ....

....

EVPS RECORDED: ....

> WHAT TIME? ....

> WHAT ROOM/AREA? ....

SO WHAT HAPPENED? ....

....

....

....

....

....

....

....

 **LOGBOOK**

Things may move quickly during an investigation, so try to remember to write things down as soon as possible after they happen.

CASE ADDRESS: ....
....
....

DATE: .... TIME: ....

ROOM OR LOCATION: ....

HOW LONG DID IT LAST? ....

WHO WAS WITH YOU? ....
....

WAS IT COLD OR HOT AT THE TIME? ....

DID YOU SMELL ANYTHING? ....
....

DID YOU FEEL ANYTHING? ....
....

DID YOU HEAR ANYTHING? ....

....

WHAT EQUIPMENT DID YOU USE? ....

....

PHOTOS TAKEN IN WHAT ROOM/AREA? ....

 › WHAT TIME? ....

 › WHAT WERE THE WEATHER CONDITIONS, IF OUTSIDE? ....

   ....

EVPS RECORDED: ....

 › WHAT TIME? ....

 › WHAT ROOM/AREA? ....

SO WHAT HAPPENED? ....

....

....

....

....

....

....

....

INTERVIEW QUESTIONNAIRE

DATE: ....

TIME: ....

WHO IS IN THE HOUSE WHEN IT OCCURS? ....

....

WHAT HAPPENED? ....

....

HAS THIS HAPPENED BEFORE? ....

RECORD SMELLS/SIGHTS/SOUNDS/FEELINGS: ....

....

NAME: ....

ADDRESS: ....

CONTACT INFORMATION—EMAIL, PHONE: ....

....

PEOPLE LIVING IN THE HOUSE WHO HAVE A PULSE AND
THEIR AGES: ....

....

PETS AND AGES: ....

....

FORMER OWNERS (IF KNOWN): ....

AGE OF HOUSE: ....

HOW LONG HAVE YOU LIVED IN THE HOUSE? ....

WHERE DID YOU LIVE BEFORE? ....

DID YOU EXPERIENCE ANY PARANORMAL ACTIVITY IN OTHER
LOCATIONS? ....

WHAT'S THE HISTORY OF THE AREA? BATTLEFIELDS NEARBY?
ANY TRAUMATIC EVENTS? ....

IS THE HOUSE ITSELF ASSOCIATED WITH TRAUMA? DEATHS?
VIOLENCE? ....

HAS THERE BEEN ANY REMODELING TO THE HOUSE, SUCH AS NEW
ROOMS, A LOT OF LANDSCAPING OUTSIDE, OR CONSTRUCTION
NEARBY? ....

HAS ANYONE OUTSIDE OF THE HOMEOWNERS EXPERIENCED
ANYTHING WHILE VISITING? ....

NAMES/CONTACT INFORMATION: ....

WHAT KIND OF ACTIVITY HAS THE FAMILY EXPERIENCED? DESCRIBE
WHEN AND WHERE: ....

HAS ANYONE FELT COLD OR HOT SPOTS OR A BREEZE WHEN
WINDOWS ARE SHUT? ....

DESCRIBE THE FIRST TIME YOU SAW, FELT, OR HEARD WHAT MIGHT
BE A PARANORMAL EXPERIENCE: ....
....

HAS IT HAPPENED AGAIN? ....

HOW OFTEN? ....

DOES IT CHANGE OR REPEAT ITSELF OVER AND OVER? ....

HOW DID YOU FEEL ABOUT IT? SCARED? INTERESTED? CALM?

....

DOES THE BUILDING HAVE ANY KNOWN STRUCTURAL PROBLEMS, SUCH AS BAD PIPES, CREAKY FLOORBOARDS, OR DRAFTY WINDOWS? DOES THE ELECTRICITY GO OFF/ON IN CERTAIN AREAS BUT NOT OTHERS? ....

....

IF THERE ARE PETS IN THE HOUSE, SUCH AS DOGS OR CATS, DO THEY ACT STRANGELY AND ATTACK UNSEEN VISITORS? DO THEY AVOID CERTAIN ROOMS OR ACT AFRAID WHEN YOU CAN'T SEE A THING? ....

....

HAS ANYONE BROUGHT SOMETHING OLD-BUT-NEW TO YOU INTO THE HOUSE? WHAT IS THE HISTORY OF THE PIECE (IF KNOWN)? FURNITURE? JEWELRY? ....

....

....

ARE THERE APPLIANCES SUCH AS TELEVISIONS AND RADIOS THAT TURN ON AND OFF ON THIER OWN? HOW OFTEN DOES THIS HAPPEN? ....

....

....

➡ FOR FURTHER READiNG

I love a good book on ghosts! Below are a few of my favorites, but don't forget to check out your local bookstore and library for a great selection of spooky titles.

Denning, Hazel M. *True Hauntings: Spirits with a Purpose*. St. Paul, MN: Llewellyn Publications, 1996.

Hauck, Dennis William. *The International Directory of Haunted Places: Ghostly Abodes, Sacred Sites, and Other Supernatural Locations*. New York: Penguin, 2000.

Holzer, Hans. *Ghosts: True Encounters with the World Beyond*. New York: Black Dog & Leventhal, 1997.

Mercado, Elaine. *Grave's End: A True Ghost Story*. St. Paul, MN: Llewellyn Publications, 2001.

Okonowicz, Ed. *Possessed Possessions: Haunted Antiques, Furniture, and Collectibles*. Elkton, MD: Myst and Lace, 1996.

Rule, Leslie. *Coast to Coast Ghosts: True Stories of Hauntings across America*. Kansas City, MO: Andrews McMeel, 2001.

Steiger, Brad. *Real Ghosts, Restless Spirits, and Haunted Places*. Canton, MI: Visible Ink, 2003.

Willin, Melvyn J. *Ghosts Caught on Film: Photographs of the Paranormal*. Newton Abbot, UK: David & Charles, 2009.

WEBSITES THAT MAKE YOU GO WHOOOOO

The Internet is chock-full of ghostly goodness, so get your research groove on, and find out more about your town's haunted past—plus some great ghost tours and paranormal investigators!

The Shadowlands: theshadowlands.net/ghost

Ghost Village: ghostvillage.com

The Ghost Research Society: ghostresearch.org

The Atlantic Paranormal Society (TAPS): the-atlantic-paranormal-society.com

The Society for Psychical Research (United Kingdom): spr.ac.uk

The American Society for Psychical Research: aspr.com

The Colorado Springs Paranormal Association: cspa.com

Ghosts of Staunton: ghostsofstaunton.com

Barb Mallon, Medium: barbmallon.com

Allegheny Paranormal: alleghenyparanormal.com

And you can visit me on the Web! Pop in and say howdy!

The Girls' Ghost Hunting Guide: girlsghosthuntingguide.com

GGHG on Facebook: facebook.com/girlsghosthuntingguide

Ask a Ghost Hunter: askaghosthunter.blogspot.com

 **BiBLiOGRAPHY**

Books

Aveni, Anthony F. *Behind the Crystal Ball: Magic, Science, and the Occult from Antiquity through the New Age.* New York: Times Books, 1996.

Buckland, Raymond. *Solitary Séance: How You Can Talk with Spirits on Your Own.* Woodbury, MN: Llewellyn Publications, 2011.

Cunningham, Scott, and David Harrington. *The Magical Household: Spells & Rituals for the Home.* St. Paul, MN: Llewellyn Publications, 2003.

Ellis, Melissa M. *The Everything Ghost Hunting Book.* Avon, MA: Adams Media, 2009.

Gibson, Marley, Patrick Burns, and Dave Schrader. *The Other Side: A Teen's Guide to Ghost Hunting and the Paranormal.* Boston: Houghton Mifflin Harcourt, 2009.

Ogden, Tom. *The Complete Idiot's Guide to Ghosts and Hauntings.* Indianapolis, IN: Alpha, 2004.

Websites

"Animal Ghosts." Real British Ghosts. www.real-british-ghosts.com.

"Black Aggie: The Haunted History of One of America's Most Mysterious Graveyard Monuments." Troy Taylor. American Hauntings and Ghosts of the Prairie. www.prairieghosts.com/druidridge.html.

"A Brief History of Paranormal Photography." Paranormal Encyclopedia. www.paranormal-encyclopedia.com/p/photography/history.html.

"Celebrity Ghost Sightings." ABCNews.com. abcnews.go.com/Entertainment/slideshow/celebrity-ghosts-11776500.

"Fox Sisters" from *Boston Journal.* November 22, 1904. Psychic Investigator. psychicinvestigator.com/demo/FOXtx2.htm.

"The Fox Sisters: Spiritualism's Unlikely Founders." HistoryNet.com. June 12, 2006. www.historynet.com/the-fox-sisters-spiritualisms-unlikely-founders.htm.

"Ghost Hunting Dog Joins Reality Show TAPS." Roz Zurko. HULIQ. June 25, 2011. www.huliq.com/12079/ghost-hunting-dog-joins-ghost-hunters.

"Ghost Hunting Tips: Use a Compass to Measure EMF." Fiona Broome. Hollow Hill. 2006. www.hollowhill.com/guide/compass.htm.

"Ghost Hunters Dog Maddie." Tamar Love Grande. Pets Adviser. March 28, 2011. petsadviser.com/news/ghost-hunters-dog-maddie.

"Gravestone Symbolism." Grave Addiction. www.graveaddiction.com/symbol.html.

"La Llorona: A Hispanic Legend." Joe Hayes. Literacynet.org. literacynet.org/lp/hperspectives/llorona.html.

"La Llorona: Weeping Ghost of the Southwest." Kathy Weiser. Legends of America. July 24, 2011. www.legendsofamerica.com/gh-lallorona.html.

"Presidents and the Paranormal: Lincoln." Stephen Wagner. About.com. paranormal.about.com/od/trueghoststories/a/Presidents-Paranormal-Lincoln.htm.

"Real Haunted Places." Real British Ghosts. www.real-british-ghosts.com/real-haunted-places.html.

"The Screaming Skull of Burton Agnes Hall." Madame Guillotine. madameguillotine.org.uk/2010/10/31/the-screaming-skull-of-burton-agnes-hall.

"Screaming Skulls, An Introduction." Daniel Parkinson. Mysterious Britain & Ireland. www.mysteriousbritain.co.uk/hauntings/screaming-skulls-an-introduction.html.

"Spirit Photography: William Mumler." Angels & Ghosts. www.angelsghosts.com/spirit_photography_william_mumler.html.

Photographs

Couple with a Young Female Spirit. National Media Museum.

Mumler, William H. *Mrs. Mary Todd Lincoln.* 1869.

West Virginia Penitentiary, West Virginia. Personal photograph by author. 2008.

Acknowledgments

FOR MY HUSBAND, BRYAN, and our five little ghost hunters: Rowyn, Syenna, Wynter, Lily, and Vyolette, who pack my ghost kit and wait impatiently for stories of floating heads upon my return.

A special thank you to Hana K. and Breanna W. for their excellent questions and Barb Mallon, Tina Carlson, Lori Hodges, Bev Sninchak, LaMishia Allen, Susan Utley, and Marty Seibel for their crackerjack ghost hunting skills. A big thank you to my agent, Dawn Frederick, for her help and cupcake bribery, and to Melanie Hooyenga, Aly Ottomeier, and Jason Tudor for being a part of the shenanigans.